A Strand of Dharma Jewels

The initial publication and short-run printing of this book have been enabled by a generous donation from Upasaka Guo Ke.

A Note on the Proper Care of Dharma Materials

Traditional Buddhist cultures treat books on Dharma as sacred. Hence it is considered disrespectful to place them in a low position, to read them when lying down, or to place them where they might be damaged by food or drink.

A Strand *of* Dharma Jewels

A Bodhisattva's Profound Teachings
On Happiness, Liberation, and the Path

The Rāja Parikathā Ratnāvalī
Composed by Ārya Nāgārjuna for a South Indian Monarch

Tripiṭaka Master Paramārtha's Sixth-Century Edition

Translation by Bhikshu Dharmamitra

KALAVINKA PRESS
Seattle, Washington
WWW.KALAVINKAPRESS.ORG

KALAVINKA PRESS
8603 39th Ave SW
Seattle, WA 98136 USA

WWW.KALAVINKAPRESS.ORG / WWW.KALAVINKA.ORG

Kalavinka Press is associated with the Kalavinka Dharma Association, a non-profit organized exclusively for religious educational purposes as allowed within the meaning of section 501(c)3 of the Internal Revenue Code. Kalavinka Dharma Association was founded in 1990 and gained formal approval in 2004 by the United States Internal Revenue Service as a 501(c)3 non-profit organization to which all donations are tax deductible.

Donations to KDA are accepted by mail and on the Kalavinka website where numerous free Dharma translations and excerpts from Kalavinka publications are available in digital format.

Copyright © 1992–2008 Bhikshu Dharmamitra. All Rights Reserved
Edition: Ratna-SA-0508-1.0
ISBN: 978-1-935413-05-9
Library of Congress Control Number: 2009920873

PUBLISHER'S CATALOGING-IN-PUBLICATION DATA

Nagarjuna, 2nd c.

[Bao hang wang zheng lun / Rāja parikathā ratnāvalī. English translation.]
A Strand of Dharma Jewels. A Bodhisattva's Profound Teachings on Happiness, Liberation, and the Path.
Translated by Bhikshu Dharmamitra. – 1st ed. – Seattle, WA: Kalavinka Press, 2009.

p. ; cm.
ISBN: 978-1-935413-05-9
Includes: stanza directory; outline; facing-page Chinese source text in both traditional and simplified scripts; appendix; notes.

1. Mādhyamika (Buddhism)—Early works to 1800. 2. Bodhisattvas. 3. Spiritual life—Mahayana Buddhism. I. Title

2009920873
0902

Cover and interior designed and composed by Bhikshu Dharmamitra.

Dedicated to the memory of the selfless and marvelous life of the Venerable Dhyāna Master Hsuan Hua, the Weiyang Ch'an Patriarch and the very personification of the Bodhisattva Path.

Dhyāna Master Hsuan Hua
宣化禪師
1918–1995

Acknowledgments

The accuracy and readability of of these first ten books of translations have been significantly improved with the aid of extensive corrections, preview comments, and editorial suggestions generously contributed by Bhikkhu Bodhi, Jon Babcock, Timothy J. Lenz, Upasaka Feng Ling, Upasaka Guo Ke, Upāsikā Min Li, and Richard Robinson. Additional valuable editorial suggestions and corrections were offered by Bhikshu Huifeng and Bruce Munson.

The initial publication and short-run printing of the initial set of ten translation volumes have been assisted by substantial donations to the Kalavinka Dharma Association by Bill and Peggy Brevoort, Freda Chen, David Fox, Upāsaka Guo Ke, Chenping and Luther Liu, Sunny Lou, Jimi Neal, and "Leo L." (a.k.a. *Camellia sinensis folium*). Additional helpful donations were offered by Doug Adams, Diane Hodgman, Bhikshu Huifeng, Joel and Amy Lupro, Richard Robinson, Ching Smith, and Sally and Ian Timm.

Were it not for the ongoing material support provided by my late guru's Dharma Realm Buddhist Association and the serene translation studio provided by Seattle's Bodhi Dhamma Center, creation of this translation would have been immensely more difficult.

Most importantly, it would have been impossible for me to produce this translation without the Dharma teachings provided by my late guru, the Weiyang Ch'an Patriarch, Dharma teacher, and exegete, the Venerable Master Hsuan Hua.

Citation and Romanization Protocols

Kalavinka Press *Taisho* citation style adds text numbers after volume numbers and before page numbers to assist rapid CBETA digital searches.

Romanization, where used, is Pinyin with the exception of names and terms already well-recognized in Wade-Giles.

The Chinese Text

This translation is supplemented by inclusion of Chinese source text on verso pages in both traditional and simplified scripts. Taisho-supplied variant readings from other editions are presented as Chinese endnotes.

This Chinese text and its variant readings are from the April, 2004 version of the Chinese Buddhist Electronic Text Association's digital edition of the Taisho compilation of the Buddhist canon.

Those following the translation in the Chinese should be aware that Taisho scripture punctuation is not traceable to original editions, is often erroneous and misleading, and is probably best ignored altogether. (In any case, accurate reading of Classical Chinese does not require any punctuation at all.)

General Table of Contents

Acknowledgements	6
Citation and Romanization Protocols	6
About the Chinese Text	6
Directory to Chapter Subsections	9
Introduction	17
The Translation: *A Strand of Jewels as Advice for the King*	31
Chapter 1: On Gaining Happiness and Liberation	31
Chapter 2: Advice on Various Topics	63
Chapter 3: The Provisions for Gaining Enlightenment	93
Chapter 4: Guidance Especially for Rulers	123
Chapter 5: On Right Practice for Monastics	157
Appendix: 57 Faults to be Abandoned	191
Endnotes	193
Source Text Variant Readings	229
About the Translator	237

Directory to Chapter Subsections
(All outlining and section titles except main chapter titles originate with the translator.)

I. **Chapter 1: On Happiness and Liberation** — 31
  A. Declaration of Homage — 31
  B. The Intent in Composing This Work — 31
  C. The Topics and Their Sequence — 31
    1. Definitions and Causes of Happiness and Liberation — 31
      a. The Roles of Faith and Wisdom — 31
        1) A Description of Superior-Grade Faith — 33
        2) The Defining Basis of Wisdom — 33
  D. The Causes of Happiness — 33
    1. Deeds to Be Avoided; Deeds to Be Cultivated — 33
      a. The Ten Evil Deeds to be Avoided — 33
      b. Deeds to Be Cultivated — 33
      c. The Uselessness of Non-beneficial Asceticism — 33
      d. The Negative Fruits of the Ten Evils and Related Transgressions — 35
    2. Summation on the Causality of Suffering and Happiness — 37
  E. The Causes of Liberation — 37
    1. The Abstruseness of Liberation's Dharmas — 37
      a. The Non-existence of "Self" — 39
      b. The World's Origin in the Imagining of "Self" and Its Possessions — 39
        1) When Perceived in Accord with Reality, Such False Conceptions Cease — 39
        2) The Aggregates Originate with Attachment to Self — 39
        3) Reality-Based Perception of Aggregates Defeats Self-grasping View — 39
        4) Analogy: Aggregates Like Mirror, "Self" Like an Unreal Reflected Image — 39
          a) The Aggregates Reflect a False Image of "Self" — 41
          b) Releasing the Aggregate "Mirror," the "Reflection" of Self Ceases — 41
          c) Ānanda's Acquisition of the Dharma Eye via This Analogy — 41
        5) Attachment to the Aggregates Ensures Continuation of Cyclic Existence — 41
        6) Twirling Firebrand Analogy: Cyclic Existence Is a Continuous Cycle — 41
        7) Cessation of Self-Imputing View Entails the End of Karma-Bound Action — 41
        8) Understanding of Origination and Cessation Halts Extreme Views — 43
        9) The Foolish Needlessly Fear This Dharma — 43
        10) Since You Don't Fear a Future Nirvāṇa, Why Fear "Emptiness"? — 43
        11) Since Non-Self Is Inevitable in Nirvāṇa, Why Fear it Now? — 43
        12) The Incompatibility of Extreme Views and Nirvāṇa — 43
    2. Definition of Wrong View and Its Disastrous Effects — 43

3.	Definition of Right View and Its Auspicious Effects	45
4.	Wisdom's Preeminence Over Dualities and Its Generation of Liberation	45
a.	The Wise Relinquish Attachment to Asserting Non-existence or Existence	45
b.	The Unreality of Production and Both Prior and Concurrent Cause	45
c.	The Fallaciousness of Polarity and Interdependency-Based Designations	45
d.	Conditioned Arising Counters Nihilism; Realism's Roots in Delusion	47
e.	Realization of True Suchness, Non-attachment, and Non-dual Liberation	47
5.	Mirage Analogy for the World, Self, Aggregates, and Dharmas	47
a.	Perceptibility of Forms Contrasted With Imperceptibility of a Mirage	47
b.	The Unreality of the World	47
c.	Refutation of the Reality of the Five Aggregates	47
d.	Clinging to Illusion as Indicative of Foolishness	47
e.	Clinging to Reality of the World is Foolish and Prevents Liberation	49
6.	Polar Attachments Beget Saṃsāra; Reality Cognition Begets Liberation	49
a.	Refutation: Disinclination to Attachment Does Not Entail Nihilism	49
7.	The Uniqueness of Buddhism's Transcendence of Dual Concepts	49
8.	Unreality of Three Times and Three Marks (Arising, Abiding, Destruction)	51
9.	On Constant Instant-by-Instant Destruction and Change	51
10.	Deconstruction of Instants and Refutation of the World's Abiding	51
11.	Deconstruction of Unitary Entities; dependence of Dual Designations	53
12.	As "Existence" Is a Fallacy, How Could any Entity Become "Non-existent"?	53
13.	Recondite Dharma and the Common Person's Misapprehension of It.	53
a.	Non-existence of the World and Nirvāṇa and the Buddha's Silence	53
b.	Recondite Dharmas Were Not Discussed with Those Unfit	53
c.	The Absence of Dependencies in Buddha's Profound Dharmas	53
d.	The Worldly, Frightened by Transcendent Dharma, Fall to Ruin	55
e.	Having Met Ruin Themselves, Be Warned: They Visit Ruin on Others	55
f.	Through Truth, One Avoids Inverted Views and Attachments	55
g.	This Teaching is Profound, Unsuited for Those Clinging to the Superficial	55
14.	Refutation of Inherent Existence in the Six Elements	55
a.	Dismissal of the Aggregates as Constituting a Self	57
15.	Analysis of the Sense Objects, Realms, and Causal Chain Is Similar	59
16.	So Too an Agent, Karma, Phenomena, Cause-and-Effect, Designations, etc.	59
17.	Wisdom Demolishes Elements, Dualities, Good, Evil, Words, etc.	59
a.	This Wisdom Extends Everywhere, Demolishing Everything	59
II. Chapter 2: Advice on Various Topics		63
A. Analogy: The "Person" is as Insubstantial as the Plantain		63
B. The Buddha Declared the Absence of any Inherent Existence in Dharmas		63
1.	The Buddha Disallowed Both Existence and Non-existence of "Self"	63
2.	So Too in the Case of Duality-Based Designations	63
3.	The Rationale for the Buddha's Remaining Silent	65
4.	Challenge: The Buddha Erred in Declaring Beings Boundlessly Many	65
5.	Response: Not So. The World Is Illusory, Transcends Dual Concepts, etc.	65

Contents

    C. As obvious Teachings Aren't Easily Absorbed, It's Truer Yet of Subtleties   67
    D. Hence the Buddha Initially Refrained from Proclaiming the Dharma   67
    E. Misunderstanding Dharma May Even Lead to One's Downfall   67
       1. Analogy: As in the Right or Wrong Use of Superior Food and Drink   69
    F. The Wise Avoid Slander of Right Dharma and Wrong Attachments   69
    G. Failing to Understand this Dharma Perpetuates Cyclic Existence   69
    H. Direct Instructions to the King   69
       1. One Must Persevere in the Perfections   69
       2. The Dharma Should Be One's Priority in the Beginning, Middle, and End   69
          a. Dharma Ensures Reputation, Happiness, Fearlessness, and Future Felicity   71
       3. Dharma is the Essence of Right and Successful Governance   71
       4. Actions Contrary to Dharma Are Wrong Governance and Beget Disaster   71
       5. Relinquishing of Faults and Emulation of Goodness Distress Adversaries   71
       6. Use Four Means of Attraction to Draw Followers and Spread Dharma   71
       7. The Four Foundations of Meritorious Qualities   73
          a. The King Should Realize "Truth" Generates Trust; Lies Diminish It   73
          b. "Relinquishment" Counters Royal Faults; Miserliness Damages Virtue   73
          c. "Stillness" Elicits Esteem; A Brilliant King Governs from Deep Serenity   73
          d. "Wisdom" Makes the King Immovable, Independent, and Undeceivable   73
          e. These Four Bases of Meritorious Qualities Engender Goodness and Praise   73
       8. Additional Practical Advice for the King   75
          a. Developing Wisdom Through Humility, Purity, Wisdom, and Compassion   75
          b. On the Rarity of Swiftly Changing to What Is Good   75
          c. On the Need to Contemplate Impermanence   75
          d. On the Negative Effects of Intoxicants   75
          e. On the Negative Effects of Gaming and Entertainments   77
          f. On Countering Lust through Realizing Impurity of the Body   77
          g. On the Negative Effects, Aspects, and Futility of Lust   81
          h. On the Disastrous Karmic Effects of Hunting   83
          i. On the Need to Relinquish Evil and Cultivate Good for the Sake of Bodhi   83
          j. On the Bases for the Realization of Bodhi in Compassion and Wisdom   83
          k. On the Causes for Gaining the Thirty-two Marks   83
          l. On the Eighty Subsidiary Physical signs   89
          m. On the Similar Marks But Deficient Causes of Wheel-Turning Sage Kings   89

III. Chapter 3: The Provisions for Gaining Enlightenment   93
    A. The Immense Merit Required for Enlightenment   93
    B. The Form Body Arises from Merit, the Dharma Body from Wisdom   95
    C. Hence the Correct Causes of Buddhahood are Merit and Wisdom   95
       1. One Should Not Be Discouraged by the Amount of Merit Required   97
          a. Beings Beset by Suffering Are Boundlessly Many   97
          b. The Bodhisattva Vows to Liberate the Countless Beings   97
          c. Immeasurable Merit Flows from this Vow   97
          d. Bodhisattva Sufferings Are Melted Away by Causal-Ground Practices   99
          e. The Wise Are Not Discouraged by the Length of the Endeavor   99

f. The Three Poisons and the Effects of Indulging or Abandoning Them	99
g. Causal-Ground Bodhisattva Practices and their Positive Effects	101
1) Facilitation of the Establishment of Dharma	101
2) Facilitation of Education	103
3) Promote Medicine, Science, Agriculture, Welfare, Emergency Services	103
4) Easing the Hardship of Travel	103
5) Establishment of Temples, Rest Pavilions, Inns	103
6) Aid to the Sick, the Poor, the Lower Classes	105
7) Food Offerings to the Religious Community and the Needy	105
8) Stocking of Temples, Rest Pavilions, and Inns with Appropriate supplies	105
9) Compassionate Treatment Even of Animals, Insects, Ghosts, etc.	105
10) On Giving	109
a) On Royal Giving Through Facilitating Marriages	109
b) Shakyamuni Buddha's Causal-Ground Precedent	109
c) On Gifts Enhancing the Ceremony	109
11) On Assisting the Worthy and Dealing with the Unworthy	109
12) On Supporting, Listening to, and Giving Right Dharma	111
13) Prefer Transcendence to Praise; Require Fine Qualities in Friends	111
14) Cultivate Three Kinds of Wisdom; Generously Repay the Guru's Kindness	111
15) Don't Study Non-Buddhist Treatises; Don't Indulge in Self-Praise	111
16) Observe Right Speech; Repent Transgressions Against Others	111
17) On the Necessity of Abandoning Faults	113
18) On Restraint from Hatred and Vengefulness	113
19) On the Need for Kindness Without Expectation of Requital	113
20) On the Need to Avoid Arrogance and Indulgence in Self-Pity	113
21) On Uncompromising Dedication to Truthfulness	113
22) On Consistency, Dedication to Goodness and Their Benefits	113
23) On Planning, Principled Actions, and Direct Knowledge of Realities	115
24) On the Fragility of Life and the Need for Dedication to Goodness	115
25) On the Auspiciousness Flowing from Reliance on Dharma	115
26) The Nine Causes for Becoming Ruler of the Gods	115
27) The Merit-Generating Power and Ten Marvelous Effects of Kindness	117
28) The Merit-Generating Power of Inspiring Resolve to Gain Enlightenment	117
29) The Important Bodhisattva Qualities & Practices and Their Effects	117
a) Faith, Moral Virtue, Emptiness, Consistent Goodness	117
b) Non-Deviousness, Contemplation, Reverence, Dharma-Protection	117
c) Facilitating Others' Access to Dharma	119
30) Non-Covetousness, Non-Miserliness, Non-Arrogance, Dharmas-Patience	119
31) Five Types of Genuine Giving and Associated Giving of Fearlessness	119
32) Causes Generating the Six Superknowledges	119
a) Causes Generating the Heavenly Eye	119
b) Causes Generating the Heavenly Ear	119
c) Causes Generating Knowledge of Others' Thoughts	119
d) Causes Generating Psychic Power	121
e) Causes Generating Knowledge of Past Lives	121
f) Causes Generating Cessation of Outflow Impurities	121
33) Compassion and Wisdom as Causes of Bodhi and Liberation of Beings	121

Contents

    34) Vows as Causes for Pure Buddhaland; Jewels as Causes of radiance   121
    35) Encouragement to Cultivate the Bodhisattva's Benefit of Others   121

IV. Chapter 4: Guidance Especially for Rulers   123

  A. Nāgārjuna's Introduction to His Instructions   123

    1. Difficulties Specific to Rulers   123

      a. Unreliability of Underlings   123
      b. Disinclination to Accept Remonstrative Teaching   123
      c. My Motivation in Offering Advice   123
      d. The Buddha's Standard for Correctness of Instruction   123
      e. The Ideal Stance for a Recipient of Teachings   123
      f. Good and Beneficial Teaching Should Be Accepted for the Sake of All   125

  B. The Instructions Proper   125

    1. On the Importance of Giving and Accomplishing Great Endeavors   125

      a. Giving As the Cause of Present Wealth; Greed As the Cause of Its Loss   125
      b. Present Giving As the Cause of Future Ease   125
      c. Exhortation to Great Resolve, Great Endeavors, Great Future Results   125

        1) Encouragement to Undertake Fine Endeavors Guided by the Three Jewels   125

          a) On the Need for Right Motivation in One's Endeavors   125
          b) On the Need to Select Endeavors Carefully   127

    2. On the Correct and Timely Uses of Wealth   127

      a. On How One May Ensure Future-Life Affluence   127
      b. On Death's Severance of the Benefits of Possessions   127
      c. Wealth's Role in Present or Future Happiness   127
      d. Why Waiting till the End to Give Won't Work   127
      e. Given the Inevitability of Death, Be Devoted to Propagating Dharma   127

    3. On Correct Governance Policies   129

      a. On Maintenance of Pre-Existing Merit-Generating Establishments   129
      b. On the Character of Stewards of Such Establishments   129
      c. On Fairness in Attendance and in Distribution of Food   129
      d. On Fairness in Bestowing Offerings on Practitioners of the Path   129
      e. On the Character of Those Facilitating Dharma-Related Endeavors   129
      f. On Character and Competence of Ministers, Officials, and Such   131
      g. On Character, Competencies, and Treatment of Financial Officials   131

    4. On Correct Motivation and Actions as King   133

      a. How the Throne May Generate the Most Supreme Benefit   133
      b. Dependence of People and King; Establishing Both dharma and Throne   133
      c. Those Whom the King Should Entrust with Oversight of His Affairs   133
      d. On Judicious Kindness and Compassion toward Detainees   133

        1) Those Who Have Been Sentenced to Restraints or Flogging   133
        2) On the Need for Compassion Even Toward the Extremely Evil   133
        3) On Limiting Length of Detention, Especially as Regards the Poor   135
        4) On Negative Effects of Indefinite Detention and Ignoring Rights   135
        5) On Providing Basic Comforts to Prisoners   135

6)	On Compassion and Bias-Free Attitude toward Good and Evil Detainees	135
7)	For the Incorrigible, Prefer Banishment to Torture or Execution	135
e.	On Security Monitoring of Activities Even of One's Own Clan	135
f.	On Commending Meritorious Service	137
g.	The Ruler's Giving Rewards: Like a Fruit-Bearing Shade Tree and Birds	137
5.	Personal Practices Affecting Governance	137
a.	Morality, Giving, and Majesty, Like a Uniquely Flavorful Confection	137
b.	The Importance of Remaining Grounded in Path-Concordant Principles	137
c.	The Fragility of the Throne and Its Basis in Dharma	137
d.	Kingship Like a Merchant Dealing in Either Suffering or Royal Privilege	137
6.	On Limits and Illusoriness of Available Pleasures at any Given Moment	139
a.	The Limited Scope of Bliss: Physical and Mental. All Else Is False	139
b.	Physical Bliss Is But Lessened Pain, Mental Bliss Is Merely A Perception	139
c.	This Being So, All Worldly Pleasures Are Devoid of Reality	139
d.	Though Possessions Are Multifarious, One Can Focus on Only One Thing	139
7.	Wisdom-Instilling Contemplations Refuting All Aspects of "Pleasure"	141
a.	When One Refrains from Sense-Object Discriminations, No Bliss Arises	141
b.	Sense Faculties and Objects Not Focused On Are Just Then Meaningless	141
c.	Mind Seizes on the Past, Discriminates, Perceives, and Imagines "Bliss"	141
d.	Mind as Subject and Sense Datum as Object Exist in Different Times	141
e.	Refutation of False Conceptions Regarding Reality of Sense Experience	141
8.	The Grave Karmic Error of Those Who Slander the Great Vehicle	145
9.	On the Defensibility of Enduring Sufferings in Spiritual Cultivation	147
10.	On the Great Vehicle's Nature and the Unjustifiability of Disparaging It	149
11.	Factors Unique to the Great Vehicle	153
12.	The Buddha's Rationale in Setting Forth Different Teachings	153
13.	Concluding Discussion on Cultivating the Great Vehicle	155
V. Chapter 5: On Right Practice for Monastics		157
A. The First Priority: Study of the Moral Codes		157
B. Next, Eliminating the Fifty-Seven Coarse Faults		157
C. Additional Practices: The Perfections, Compassion, Related Dharmas		169
1.	The Perfections and Compassion	169
2.	On the Ten Bodhisattva Grounds	169
a.	The First Ground: The Ground of Joyfulness	169
b.	The Second Ground: The Ground of Non-Defilement	171
c.	The Third Ground: The Ground of Illumination	171
d.	The Fourth Ground: The Ground of Flaming Intelligence	173
e.	The Fifth Ground: The Ground of Being Difficult to Overcome	173
f.	The Sixth Ground: The Ground of Direct Facing	173
g.	The Seventh Ground: The Ground of Being Far-Reaching	175
h.	The Eighth Ground: The Kumāra Ground, the Ground of Immovability	175
i.	The Ninth Ground: The Ground of Fine Intelligence	177
j.	The Tenth Ground: The Ground of the Dharma Cloud	177
3.	The Ground of Buddhahood	177

4. TWENTY VERSES TO GENERATE THE CAUSES AND RESULT OF BUDDHAHOOD   179
5. THE MERIT OF SUCH CULTIVATION IS INCALCULABLE   185
6. CONCLUDING INSTRUCTIONS   185

Introduction

Introductory Notes on This Text

A Strand of [Dharma] Jewels as Advice for the King (*Rāja-parikathā-ratnāvalī*) is a 500-stanza treatise on Mahāyāna right view, practice, and realization written by Ārya Nāgārjuna sometime in the late first quarter of the first millennium CE. Although it is presented in the form of a letter to a monarch setting forth advice on how best to achieve happiness and gain liberation while also governing for the highest good of both king and country, its intent extends far beyond that: It is a reasonably complete guide for those aspiring to bodhisattva practice on how to understand the mind and the world, how to think and act in the world, and how to achieve the highest realization of mind in transcending the world, even while working all the while for universal good in the world.

The edition from which this English translation is made is the Sanskrit-to-Chinese translation produced by the Indian Tripiṭaka Master Paramārtha (499–569 CE) during the early years of the Ch'en dynasty (557–589 CE). Paramārtha was an Indian monk of Brahman-caste origins from Ujjain, the famous and historic city in Madhya Pradesh. He is revered as one of the greatest translators in the history of Chinese Buddhism.

General Discussion of the Author and the Text

The author of this treatise, Ārya Nāgārjuna, is recognized by followers of all Northern School Buddhist traditions as one of the foremost advocates of the Mahāyāna path dedicated to universal spiritual liberation and realization of buddhahood. Nāgārjuna championed this path as of a higher order than the individual-liberation paths idealizing personal escape from suffering through the enlightenment of arhats or pratyekabuddhas.

We have biographies of Nāgārjuna in both Chinese and Tibetan traditions varying widely in the degree of hagiographic content. Of course there has also been much discussion about the life of Nāgārjuna in the academic literature as well as in the secondary literature emanating from Western Buddhist faith communities.[1] Still, when all is said and done, we don't actually know very much for certain about any concrete details regarding Nāgārjuna's life either before or after he became a monk.

Obviously, much can be deduced about the character of Nāgārjuna's thought through studying the texts he is supposed to have authored. If we focus solely on those texts for which Nāgārjunian authorship is generally acknowledged, we notice right away several standard features: a) an emphasis on emptiness teachings so thorough-going that they dismiss inherent existence of any and all phenomena; b) a predilection for the use of *reductio ad absurdum* dialectics seizing on the Achilles heel of any proposition positing inherent existence; and c) extremely consistent promotion of universal-liberation doctrines along with all of their subsidiary practices such as Mahāyāna enlightenment resolve, the great compassion, and dedication to the Bodhisattva Path.

But, as one might expect, the question of precisely which texts were actually composed by Ārya Nāgārjuna is a matter of ongoing debate. In this debate, there seem to be two equally incredible extremes framing a moderately reasonable middle ground. At the one extreme, we have a tiny minority of modern authors who will admit Nāgārjuna wrote the *Treatise on the Middle* while refusing to believe any Mahāyāna writings ever issued from his hand. At the other extreme, we have from among the Tibetan faith community a substantial number of individuals convinced that, above and beyond his authorship of the *Treatise on the Middle* and numerous Mahāyāna texts, Nāgārjuna lived over 500 years in a single human body and was a practitioner of tantra as well.

Setting aside the extremes for a moment, there does seem to be general middle-ground agreement on Nāgārjuna's authorship of *The Treatise on the Middle, The Twelve-Gate Treatise, Seventy Verses on Emptiness, Sixty Verses on Reasoning, Letter from a Friend, Provisions for Enlightenment, Analytic Treatise on the Ten Grounds, Strand of Jewels,* and a number of other texts.

Opinions vary considerably on other works such as *Commentary on the Great Perfection of Wisdom Sutra* towards which doubts have been raised, but only on the basis of merely external circumstantial evidence. (The few negative internal-evidence arguments are easily refuted, for which see my essay on the matter.)

The *Sūtrasamuccaya* may be another "grey-area" text in the eyes of some observers As much as I loved reading the *Sūtrasamuccaya*, I find its tenor markedly different from anything else I've read from

Nāgārjuna and hence, absent further evidence, I am forced into agnosticism on questions regarding its authorship.

Mainstream secular buddhology has also found some difficulty in concurring with the Tibetan historical tradition's ascribing to the original *Middle Treatise* Nāgārjuna authorship of texts referencing consciousness-only schools (as with the *Bodhicittavivaraṇa*) or tantra (as with the *Pañcakrama*). David Seyfort Ruegg, for example, suggests these two works were composed by a seventh-century eminence, a "Nāgārjuna II," who happened to carry the same name. (*The Literature of the Madhyamaka School*, p. 104-5.)

Although there does not seem to be any particular controversy about the validity of attributing authorship of this *Strand of Jewels* text to Nāgārjuna, interpretations vary as to precisely which king was the intended recipient of its teachings. Nāgārjuna makes clear in the text itself that he wrote it not just for the benefit of the king, but rather for the benefit of all beings in the future who would take up cultivation of the Mahāyāna path of liberation.

Students of Nāgārjuna will of course already be familiar with a similar text generally acknowledged as authored by the same eminence, namely *Letter from a Friend* (*Suhṛllekha*). The two texts differ markedly in the depth of content, perhaps largely from the fact that this *Strand of Jewels* text is roughly five times greater in length. From internal evidence, though, one might well suppose that *Letter from a Friend* was written for an entirely different monarch (or the same monarch at an earlier age), one with a seemingly less sophisticated level of intellectual development or present-life spiritual aptitude. (The Chinese edition translated by Tripiṭaka Master Guṇavarman states that the *Suhṛllekha* was written by Ārya Nāgārjuna for the benefit of a King Śatakarṇī, one of a number of identically-named Sātavāhana rulers who occupied the throne in Amaravati.)

Those wishing to explore these two distinctly different "royal advisory" texts may choose to explore my translation of the three earliest editions of *Letter from a Friend* (translated by Tripiṭaka Masters Guṇavarman, Saṅghavarman, and Yijing) which I am publishing under a single separate cover. (Alternatively, there are widely-available translations from the much-later Tibetan edition.)

On the Title

There are minor variations in the recorded Sanskrit title of this work. Apparently the single partial surviving Sanskrit copy datable to the nineteenth century refers to it as the *Ratnāvalī*, whereas the Tibetan translation edition "rewritten" in roughly 1100 CE transliterates the title as *Rāja-parikathā-ratnamālā*.

The Chinese edition is datable at the latest from 569 CE. This corresponds to the end of the life of the translator Tripiṭaka Master Paramārtha. One may justify from the meaning of the translated Chinese title (寶行王正論) the fairly obvious reconstruction as *Rāja-parikathā-ratnāvalī* (*bao*-3 *hang*-2 / 寶行 = *ratnāvalī*; *wang*-2 *zheng*-4 *lun*-4 / 王正論 = *rāja-parikathā*).

Given that a *rāja-parikathā* is "a discourse advising the king," and "*ratnāvalī*" is "a strand of jewels," it is clear that we are dealing with a discourse consisting of Dharma truths presented to a king, likened by analogy to a strand or necklace of jewels, or (in the case of the Tibetan edition's transliteration as "*ratnamālā*") likened by analogy to prayer beads made of jewels. The obvious intent of the title is to liken the teachings contained in the discourse advising the king to an artfully arranged strand of jewels.

The most common English translation chosen so far for the Tibetan edition ("Precious Garland of Advice for the King") apparently involves either an artifact of the Tibetan words used to translate the Sanskrit title or simply a matter of the translator's creative choice in translating "*ratna* / jewel" in an adjectival sense and translating "*mālā* / necklace" in its alternative sense as a "wreath or garland," i.e. as "a wreath or festoon of flowers worn as decorative or honorific ornamentation."

On the Three Extant Editions

We have three source texts from which to derive an understanding of Ārya Nāgārjuna's *Strand of Jewels*, as follows:

a) The earliest datable text is preserved in the Taisho edition of the Chinese Buddhist canon (T32.1656.593b-505b). It is the edition translated by Tripiṭaka Master Paramārtha (500–569 CE) during the Ch'en Dynasty (557–589 CE), datable at the latest from 569 CE, the end of the life of the translator.[2]

b) The Tibetan originates with a translation made by Jñānagarbha and Klu'i rgyal mtshan, probably at the beginning of the ninth century. Due to perceived doctrinal errors in the original translation, it was revised two hundred years later by Kanakavarman and Pa tshab ñi ma grags who consulted several distinctly different Sanskrit editions in making their changes.[3]

c) The very late (nineteenth century?) fragments of the Sanskrit comprise roughly three and a half of the original five chapters. They are the only known surviving fragments of any original transmitted through a long line of Sanskrit oral transmittals and palm-leaf transcription.

There are any number of difficulties in preferring readings from any of these texts over the others. For instance, as readily as we might otherwise be inclined to favor readings from the very substantial and valuable extant Sanskrit fragments, we are given cause for pause once we stop and wonder how many merely oral transmittals were involved, how many times the written version of the text was recopied, and how many errors and corruptions in recopying the text occurred across the course of the previous 1600 years. As illustrated by our knowledge of the process involved in revising the original error-ridden Tibetan translation wherein the revisers were faced with deciding between readings in three different versions of the Sanskrit in the early eleventh century, many changes must have already been affecting the Sanskrit versions by that midway point between the texts original composition and the current partial palm-leaf copy which survives today (at least on mostly very readable microfiche).

Although the Tibetan edition originates in part from a relatively early initial translation (early ninth century?) whereby it emerged into Tibetan after perhaps six hundred years of Sanskrit transmittal, it was revised two hundred years later (i.e. not retranslated) by consulting several editions available to the revisers at the beginning of the eleventh century. The very fact that there were three distinctly different editions of the Sanskrit from which the revisionists were forced to choose in recasting what they deemed to be an unsatisfactory original translation leads one to wonder how many corruptions had already entered the text at that point and, additionally, how many new corruptions then entered the Tibetan translation as a result of consulting three differing editions while rewriting it.

Although the Chinese is the earliest edition, Hahn (in *Nāgārjuna's Ratnāvalī*) claims to have identified a number of minor corruptions in the text, most of which I feel comfortable in endorsing as factual. Additionally, it is not always so easy to deduce with precision the particular very important antecedent Sanskrit technical terms that lie behind Paramārtha's Chinese renderings. This latter problem is assisted somewhat by referencing the seventy-percent complete, but highly evolved Sanskrit fragments together with recently-available Sanskrit-Chinese concordances to other works translated by the very prolific translator of this *Ratnāvalī*, Tripiṭaka Master Paramārtha. (The reader will notice I have restored several very brief passages from Tucci's Sanskrit as emendations producing a truly complete English translation. These emendations are clearly marked in both text and notes.)

Fortunately, the Sanskrit, Chinese, and Tibetan editions track each other fairly closely and, where there are variances, they need not be interpreted as representing any genuinely contradictory pronouncements on either doctrine or practice. Where there is some minor cause for confusion in contemplating the phrasing of one edition, reflecting on the renderings found in the other editions is often very helpful in sorting out the difficulty.

One example of how one edition's statements can assist understanding another tradition's text lies in probably the most technically demanding section of the *Ratnāvalī*, the "fifty-seven faults to be abandoned" listed by Nāgārjuna in the beginning of the fifth chapter. Apparent ambiguity in the Sanskrit and Tibetan is to a certain degree clarified by referencing the Chinese text wherein Paramārtha was kind enough to use a sentence structure clearly designating and distinguishing the names of each of those faults. This artifact in Paramārtha's translation methodology helps prevent a vulnerability in reading the Sanskrit whereby definitional text may be confused with the names of the fifty-seven terms themselves.

Another example: Where problems in understanding the Chinese were made more difficult by Paramārtha's (or his editors') choosing to render very technically complex stanzas with only five characters per *śloka* foot, referencing the Sanskrit or the Tibetan has often been quite helpful in clarifying subtleties.

On the Internal Structure of the Text

The five chapters of the *Ratnāvalī* deal primarily with five main topics and secondarily with many important subtopics crucial to understanding right Mahāyāna view, practice, and realization. I outline them below only briefly:

1) The first chapter, entitled "On Gaining Happiness and Liberation" explains how to achieve realization of these two priorities in the well-lived and deeply reflective life.

As regards "happiness," noting that the preoccupation with happiness tends to be universal and foremost in the minds of worldly beings, Nāgārjuna clarifies the causes to be cultivated or avoided in bringing about realization of happiness in both present and future lives, focusing on the most pivotal of all, right ethics as embodied in the abstention from the ten types of unwholesome karma. He also points out the uselessness of non-beneficial forms of asceticism while describing as well the negative karmic fruits of indulgence in unwholesome physical, verbal, or mental karma.

In his long section discussing "liberation" which forms the deepest metaphysical core of this entire work, Nāgārjuna first speaks of right understanding of "non-self," the origin of the world in imagining a self and appurtenances of a self, and then explains how reality-based perception defeats self-grasping view. He empowers these teachings through resort to the traditional "reflection in the mirror," "twirling firebrand," and "mirage" analogies.

In the course of explaining the causes of liberation, Nāgārjuna treats a wide array of important subtopics too numerous to enumerate here, but which I have detailed extensively in the Table of Contents. They include:

Refutation of charges that denying inherent existence is somehow nihilist;
Definitions of right and wrong view and the negative consequence of non-adherence to right view;
Wisdom's role in generating liberation;
The need to relinquish clinging to views positing either existence or non-existence;
The unreality of production, prior cause, and concurrent cause;
The inherent fallaciousness of polarity-based and interdependency-based designations;
How understanding of conditioned-arising counters nihilism;
How realism is in fact rooted in delusion;
The importance of realizing true suchness, non-attachment, and non-dual liberation;
Deconstruction of the world, self, aggregates, and dharmas;
The unreality of time and the three marks of arising, abiding, and destruction;
Refutation of the reality of the four and six elements.

Suffice it to say that this discussion focusing on wisdom and liberation is key to everything else presented in this entire five-chapter presentation of right Mahāyāna view, practice, and realization. Failure to spend some deeply reflective time on these topics will prevent right understanding of the path of liberation to which Nāgārjuna has dedicated this *Strand of Jewels* discourse.

2) The second chapter, entitled "Advice on Various Topics," begins with declarations on absence of inherent existence in both persons and dharmas and continues to statements on the non-ultimacy of existence-affirming views, non-existence-affirming views, and duality-based designations.

Nāgārjuna makes the point that misunderstanding Dharma teachings can lead to one's own karmic downfall and unnecessary perpetuation of uncontrolled cyclic existence. He also counsels against slandering right Dharma teachings and coursing in erroneous attachments.

The second chapter then moves to a series of instructions on doctrine and practical action which, although not the least bit exclusively applicable to monarchs, are none the less formally addressed to the King. These include instructions on the four means of attraction used to draw people into deeper understanding of Dharma, instructions on the four foundations of meritorious qualities, and a long series of instructions on the advisability of developing wisdom, swiftly changing to what is good, contemplating impermanence, avoiding intoxicants, gambling, and frivolous entertainments, on countering any tendency to over-indulge lust, on refraining from the hunting of animals, and on relinquishing evil and cultivating good for the sake of gaining enlightenment.

Nāgārjuna then concludes the second chapter with instructions on the role of compassion and wisdom in gaining enlightenment and instructions on the causes for gaining the body of a buddha in a future life.

3) The third chapter, entitled "The Provisions for Gaining Enlightenment," as the title would suggest, is nominally dedicated to the prerequisites which the bodhisattva practitioner must complete across the course of countless lifetimes in order to ascend through all the bodhisattva stages to the ultimate realization of buddhahood.

Nāgārjuna begins the chapter with a description of the immense amount of merit required for the realization of buddhahood, notes that merit is the cause for gaining the form body of a buddha whereas wisdom is the cause for gaining the Dharma body of a buddha, and then insists that one should not be discouraged by the amount of merit required for buddhahood. He points out that the beings beset by suffering are boundlessly many, that the bodhisattva vows to liberate these countless beings, and that the very fact of making that vow itself generates boundless merit.

Next, after noting that the bodhisattva's sufferings are melted away by the causal-ground practices, Nāgārjuna emphasizes that the wise are not discouraged by the length of the endeavor and that one must pay close attention to the effects of either indulging or abandoning the three poisons. He then proceeds through an extensive catalogue of important causal-ground bodhisattva practices and their positive effects, finishing with a list of the causes generating the six superknowledges, buddhahood, the liberation of beings, and purification of the buddhaland.

Those wishing to explore the main topic of this chapter more thoroughly may care to read my complete translation of Nāgārjuna's *Bodhisaṃbhāra Śāstra* and its early Indian commentary for they are devoted exclusively to this all-important topic and discuss it in exhaustive detail.

4) The fourth chapter, entitled "Guidance Especially for Rulers," is addressed primarily to those engaged in governance even though the principles contained therein are generally useful to anyone, whether a dedicated practitioner of the Path or merely a citizen of the country. The final third of the chapter is by no means exclusive in its utility to those in positions of power.

Important topics from the latter part of the chapter certainly interesting and relevant to all Dharma practitioners include:

The limited scope and illusory nature of pleasures;
Wisdom-instilling contemplations refuting the reality of all aspects of pleasurable experiences;
The grave karmic error of those who slander the Mahāyāna;
The nature of the Mahāyāna and the unjustifiability of disparaging it in any way;
Factors unique to the Mahāyāna;
The Buddha's rationale in setting forth different teachings.

Nāgārjuna's concluding discussion on the practice of the Mahāyāna suggests to the king that matters could evolve to where practicing right Dharma and continuing to occupy the throne might become incompatible, in which case the right course of action could be to renounce the throne and become a monk.

5) The fifth and final chapter carries the mildly misleading title "On Right Practice for Monastics." (There is nothing in the entire chapter not perfectly appropriate for any practitioner of the Bodhisattva Path, whether lay or monastic.)

The chapter commences by noting that the beginning monastic pays close attention to study and practice of the monastic's moral code. It then continues with a presentation of fifty-seven faults to be abandoned. (See the Appendix for an easily perusable list.) Next we have an array of additional bodhisattva practices (the perfections, compassion, and related dharmas), and a brief listing and discussion of the Ten Bodhisattva Grounds. Nāgārjuna then concludes by setting forth twenty verses to assist generation of the causes and result of buddhahood, by pointing out that the merit of such cultivation is incalculably vast, and by summing up the treatise with final instructions.

On the Special Character and Utility of This Text

The most important feature of this text is its inclusion in a relatively short discourse all of the teachings necessary for genuinely understanding the practice of the bodhisattva as he courses along in this one life as well as in lifetime-after-lifetime of cyclic existence, assembling all the prerequisites necessary for the realization of buddhahood.

The *Strand of Jewels* is especially practical in the nature of its instructions. Thus it explains clearly how to generate merit and achieve happiness while also giving due weight to the pursuit of the wisdom which generates spiritual liberation. Great attention is given to the very specific details of personal spiritual cultivation and how to integrate them with the mundane details of worldly existence.

Finally, having provided detailed instructions on gaining happiness, pursuing liberation, assembling the causes for buddhahood, and carrying out the responsibilities of leadership, Nāgārjuna describes in brief monastic practice and long-term bodhisattva practice which in some lives will be as a layperson, and which in other lives will be as a monastic.

On Elements Added by the Translator

All headings aside from the five chapter headings are inserted by the translator to facilitate easier initial assessment and navigation of the text. Although I did not obsess on appropriateness or precision in slicing and naming sections and subsections, the outline structure probably comes close to reflecting the implicit organization of Nāgārjuna's text. Still, the reader is counseled to treat my outline apparatus as merely preliminary and advisory.

On a related note, even against the advice of a few worthy English-language partisans, I've included on verso pages the source-language texts in both simplified-character and traditional-character scripts. There are three reasons for this:

First, I think it can be helpful to Dharma students and specialists who have taken the time to develop Chinese-language skills to have ready access to the source-language in contemplating abstruse or opaque passages.

Second, there are no small number of readers who can mostly read the Chinese fairly well, but who still need a little help interpreting the code-speak of Sino-Buddhist technical terms not found anywhere in the modern Chinese lexicon. Facing-page English allows them to mostly skip the English altogether, while still having the readily-available "crutch" of my recto-page English translation as a "ready-reference" for unfamiliar or difficult technical terms.

Third, I'm fishing for critical comments on translation quality and precision to facilitate improvements in subsequent editions. Placing the source language right next to the translation enhances the possibility of inspiring a few more recommendations from readers willing to mobilize their compassion toward that end.

Finally, I've added a list of the "Fifty-seven Faults to be Abandoned," Endnotes, and "Source Text Variant Readings" to encourage deeper study and contemplation of this text.

In Summary

Ārya Nāgārjuna's *Strand of Jewels* is a marvelous presentation of the Bodhisattva Path clearly articulating the ethical restraints, virtuous endeavors, contemplative practices, and liberation methods with which the bodhisattva practitioner must develop deep understanding and competency. I feel that this discourse is such a unique and valuable resource for the serious Mahāyāna practitioner that it really should be widely circulated and studied by modern-day students of the Path.

Given that the received editions of this text do in fact demonstrate significant variations in their degree of clarity, I believe that this translation of the earliest extant edition of Nāgārjuna's *Strand of Jewels* may serve as a resource through which practitioners of the Bodhisattva Path may resolve points of ambiguity and thus better-understand Nāgārjuna's precise meaning.

I don't doubt, given the abstruseness of the text and the terseness of the Chinese source text, that there may be room for revision of this translation. Suggestions for improvements from clergy, scholars, or Dharma students may be forwarded via website email and will certainly be very much appreciated.

Bhikshu Dharmamitra.
Buddha's Birthday, 2008

A Strand of Dharma Jewels As Advice for the King

The Rāja Parikathā Ratnāvalī

Composed by Ārya Nāgārjuna

Sanskrit-to-Chinese Translation by Tripiṭaka Master Paramārtha

English Translation by Bhikshu Dharmamitra

宝行王正论[5]

[圣者龙树菩萨造]
陈天竺[6]三藏真谛译

安乐解脱品第一

1-001
解脱一切障圆德所庄严
礼一切智尊众生真善友

1-002
正法决定善为爱法大王
我当说由法流注法器人

1-003
先说乐因法后辩解脱法
众生前安乐次[7]后得解脱

1-004
善道具名乐解脱谓惑尽
略说此二因唯信智二根

1-005
因信能持法由智如实了
二中智最胜先藉信发行

寶行王正論[5]

[聖者龍樹菩薩造]
陳天竺[6]三藏真諦譯

安樂解脫品第一

1-001
解脫一切障圓德所莊嚴
禮一切智尊眾生真善友

1-002
正法決定善為愛法大王
我當說由法流注法器人

1-003
先說樂因法後辯解脫法
眾生前安樂次[7]後得解脫

1-004
善道具名樂解脫謂惑盡
略說此二因唯信智二根

1-005
因信能持法由智如實了
二中智最勝先藉信發行

Chapter One
On Gaining Happiness and Liberation

I. Chapter 1: On Happiness and Liberation
   A. Declaration of Homage

001

To he who has gained liberation from all obstacles
And is adorned with the perfected qualities—[4]
I bow in reverence to the Omniscient Honored One,[5]
The true good friend of beings.[6]

   B. The Intent in Composing This Work

002

Right Dharma, definite in its goodness,
[Is presented here] for the Dharma-cherishing Great King.
I shall explain it in a manner reliant upon Dharma,
That it may flow into a person fit to be a vessel of the Dharma.[7]

   C. The Topics and Their Sequence

003

First, I shall explain the dharmas causing happiness,
Afterwards, I shall distinguish the dharmas generating liberation.
Beings place obtaining happiness as foremost,
And then afterwards pursue liberation.

     1. Definitions and Causes of Happiness and Liberation

004

Perfection in the path of goodness defines "happiness."
"Liberation," refers to the extinguishing of delusions.
Generally speaking, the causes for these two
Lie solely in two faculties: faith and wisdom.

       a. The Roles of Faith and Wisdom

005

Due to faith, one is able to uphold the Dharma.
Through wisdom, one's comprehension accords with reality.
Of the two, wisdom is superior.
Still, one first relies on faith to initiate the practices.[8]

简体字	正體字
1-006 由痴贪瞋怖而能不坏法 当知是有信吉祥乐名器	1-006 由癡貪瞋怖而能不壞法 當知是有信吉祥樂名器
1-007 已能熟简择身口意三业 恒利益自他说为有智人	1-007 已能熟簡擇身口意三業 恒利益自他說為有智人
1-008 杀生盗邪婬妄言及两舌 恶骂不应语贪瞋与邪见	1-008 殺生盜邪婬妄言及兩舌 惡罵不應語貪瞋與邪見
1-009 此法名十恶翻此即十善 离酒清净命无逼恼心施	1-009 此法名十惡翻此即十善 離酒清淨命無逼惱心施
1-010 供养所应敬略说法当尔 若但行苦行决不生善法	1-010 供養所應敬略說法當爾 若但行苦行決不生善法
1-011 以离智悲故若唯有苦行 不能除损他与救济利益	1-011 以離智悲故若唯有苦行 不能除損他與救濟利益

1) A Description of Superior-Grade Faith

006

If someone beset by delusion, desire, hatefulness, or fear
Is nonetheless able to avoid ruining [his practice of] Dharma,
One should realize he possesses faith
And may be considered a vessel of auspicious happiness.

2) The Defining Basis of Wisdom

007

Once one has become able to be skillfully selective
In the three karmic actions of body, mouth, and mind
While also constantly benefiting self and others,
He becomes fit to be known as one who is wise.[9]

D. The Causes of Happiness
1. Deeds to Be Avoided; Deeds to Be Cultivated
a. The Ten Evil Deeds to be Avoided

008

Killing, stealing, sexual misconduct,
False speech, divisive speech,
Harsh speech, inappropriate discourse,
Covetousness, ill-will, and wrong views—

b. Deeds to Be Cultivated

009

These dharmas constitute the ten unwholesome karmic deeds.
Their opposites are just the ten good karmic deeds.
Abandoning intoxicants, adhering to pure livelihood,
Having no motivation to torment, practicing generosity,

010

And making offerings to those who should be revered—
Briefly described, one's Dharma should be of this sort.[10]

c. The Uselessness of Non-beneficial Asceticism

If one only practices ascetic disciplines,
One will definitely fail to generate the dharmas of goodness.

011

Because it involves abandonment of wisdom and compassion,
If one is exclusively devoted to ascetic disciplines,
One remains unable to do away with harming others,
And unable to provide them with rescue and benefit.

1-012
施戒修忍所明正法大夷路
若弃行邪道自苦受牛罚

1-013
是生死旷泽无饮食树阴
[8]或狼所食噉长远于中行

1-014
因杀生短寿逼恼招多病
由盗致乏财侵他境多怨

1-015
妄语[9]遭诽谤两舌亲爱离
恶口闻不爱绮语他憎嫉

1-016
由贪害所求瞋恚受惊怖
邪见生僻执饮酒心讷乱

1-017
不施故贫穷邪命逢欺诳
不恭生卑贱嫉妒无威德

1-018
10恒恨形色丑不问11聪故痴
此报在人道先已受恶趣

简体字

1-012
施戒修忍所明正法大夷路
若棄行邪道自苦受牛罰

1-013
是生死曠澤無飲食樹陰
[8]或狼所食噉長遠於中行

1-014
因殺生短壽逼惱招多病
由盜致乏財侵他境多怨

1-015
妄語[9]遭誹謗兩舌親愛離
惡口聞不愛綺語他憎嫉

1-016
由貪害所求瞋恚受驚怖
邪見生僻執飲酒心訥亂

1-017
不施故貧窮邪命逢欺誑
不恭生卑賤嫉妒無威德

1-018
10恒恨形色醜不問11聰故癡
此報在人道先已受惡趣

正體字

012
That which is illuminated by giving, moral virtue, [and patience]
Is the great and level road of right Dharma.¹¹
If one were to forsake it and course instead on an erroneous path,
Taking on oneself austerities emulating a cow's karmic torments,¹²

013
Then, in this vast wilderness swamp of cyclic birth and death,
One might course on without drink, food, or shade of trees,
And might be subject then to being devoured by wolves,
Journeying on within it for a long time and across great distances.¹³

   d. THE NEGATIVE FRUITS OF THE TEN EVILS AND RELATED TRANSGRESSIONS

014
On account of killing, one is born into short-lived existences.
By physically tormenting others, one brings on much sickness.
Through stealing, one brings about insufficiency of wealth.
Through invading another's domain, one gains many enemies.¹⁴

015
On account of lying, one is bound to encounter slander.
Through divisive speech, one is estranged from those held dear.
Because of harsh speech, one will hear what is not pleasing.
Through frivolous speech, one becomes loathed by others.¹⁵

016
Through covetousness, one brings harm to what is sought.
Due to hatefulness, one will be subjected to terror.
Because of wrong views, one generates perverse attachments.
Through drinking alcohol, the mind becomes dull and chaotic.

017
Through failure to practice giving, one falls into poverty.
On account of wrong livelihood, one encounters deceit.
Due to not being respectful, one is born into low social station.
Through jealousy, one becomes devoid of awe-inspiring qualities.

018
Through constant anger, one's appearance becomes ugly.
By failing to inquire of the intelligent, one becomes stupid.
These are retributions as they occur on the path of human rebirth,
Prior to this, one has already endured the wretched destinies.

1-019

杀生等罪法如所说果报
[*kuśalānāṃ ca sarveṣāṃ viparītaḥ phalodayaḥ*] (19c-d emended via Sanskrit.)

1-020

[*lobho dveṣaś ca mohas ca tajjaṃ karmeti cāśubham*] (20a-b via Sanskrit.)
无贪等及业说名善习因

1-021

恶修及诸苦皆从邪法生
诸善道安乐皆因善法起

1-022

常离一切恶恒行一切善
由身口意业应知此二法

1-023

由一法能脱地狱等四趣
第二法能感人天王富乐

1-024

由定梵住空得受梵等乐
如是略说名乐因及乐果

1-025

复次解脱法微细深难见
无耳心凡夫闻则生惊怖

简体字

1-019

殺生等罪法如所說果報
[*kuśalānāṃ ca sarveṣāṃ viparītaḥ phalodayaḥ*] (19c-d emended via Sanskrit.)

1-020

[*lobho dveṣaś ca mohas ca tajjaṃ karmeti cāśubham*] (20a-b via Sanskrit.)
無貪等及業說名善習因

1-021

惡修及諸苦皆從邪法生
諸善道安樂皆因善法起

1-022

常離一切惡恒行一切善
由身口意業應知此二法

1-023

由一法能脫地獄等四趣
第二法能感人天王富樂

1-024

由定梵住空得受梵等樂
如是略說名樂因及樂果

1-025

復次解脫法微細深難見
無耳心凡夫聞則生驚怖

正體字

Chapter 1: *On Gaining Happiness and Liberation*

2. SUMMATION ON THE CAUSALITY OF SUFFERING AND HAPPINESS[16]

019

The karmic-offense dharmas associated with killing and such
Involve karmic retributions such as have just been described.
[*kuśalānāṃ ca sarveṣāṃ viparītaḥ phalodayaḥ*]: (19c-d emended via Sanskrit.)
[All of the good karmic deeds
Involve karmic retributions opposite to those.][17]

020

[*lobho dveṣaś ca mohas ca tajjaṃ karmeti cāśubham*]: (20a-b via Sanskrit)
[Covetousness, hatred, and delusion
As well as karma arising from them are moral evils.]
Non-covetousness and such as well as karma arising from them
Exemplify the causality involved in good karmic actions.

021

The wretched destinies[18] and the various forms of suffering
Are all produced as a consequence of wrong dharmas.
The good destinies and happiness,
All arise because of good dharmas.

022

One should always avoid every form of evil
While constantly engaging in every form of goodness,
Doing so through the karmic actions of body, mouth, and mind.
One should abide in awareness of these two dharmas.[19]

023

By resort to the first dharma, one is able to gain freedom
From the hells and the rest of the four [unfortunate] destinies.[20]
The second of these dharmas is able to bring on
The wealth and happiness enjoyed by humans, gods, and kings.

024

Through concentrations, *brahma-vihāras*, and formless absorptions,[21]
One gains the bliss of Brahmā and the others.[22]
Thus we set forth a summary explanation of
The causes for happiness as well as their blissful karmic rewards.

E. THE CAUSES OF LIBERATION
1. THE ABSTRUSENESS OF LIBERATION'S DHARMAS

025

Additionally, there are the dharmas associated with liberation
Which are subtle, profound, and difficult to perceive.
As for the common person whose mind has no ears for them—
Were he to hear them described, he would be struck with fear.

简体字	正體字
1-026 我无当不生现来我所无 凡人思此畏智者怖永尽	**1-026** 我無當不生現來我所無 凡人思此畏智者怖永盡
1-027 世间我见生他事执所系 佛由至道证依悲为他说	**1-027** 世間我見生他事執所繫 佛由至道證依悲為他說
1-028 我有及我所此二[1]实皆虚 由见如实理二执不更生	**1-028** 我有及我所此二[1]實皆虛 由見如實理二執不更生
1-029 诸阴我执生我执由义虚 若种子不实[2]芽等云何真	**1-029** 諸陰我執生我執由義虛 若種子不實[2]芽等云何真
1-030 若见阴不实我见则不生 由我见灭尽诸阴不更起	**1-030** 若見陰不實我見則不生 由我見滅盡諸陰不更起
1-031 如人依净镜得见自面影 此影但可见一向不真实	**1-031** 如人依淨鏡得見自面影 此影但可見一向不真實

a. The Non-existence of "Self"

026

The "I" is non-existent, nor shall it arise in the future.
Anything considered "mine" is non-existent, now and in the future.
When the common person ponders this, he becomes frightened.
As for the wise—all fears are forever ended in them.

b. The World's Origin in the Imagining of "Self" and Its Possessions

027

The world is born from the view imputing existence of a "self."
One is then bound by attachment to phenomena seen as "other."
The Buddha achieved his realization based on the ultimate path.
By resort to compassion, he explained this for the sake of others.

1) When Perceived in Accord with Reality, Such False Conceptions Cease

028

The existence of a self as well as that which belongs to a self—
These two, in reality, are in all cases false.
It is through perceiving them in accordance with reality
That the two types of attachment arise no more.

2) The Aggregates Originate with Attachment to Self

029

The aggregates are generated through attachment to a self.[23]
According to the [ultimate] meaning,[24] attachment to "self" is invalid.
If the seed itself has no reality,
How could the sprout and such be grounded in truth?[25]

3) Reality-Based Perception of Aggregates Defeats Self-grasping View

030

If one perceives that the aggregates themselves are not real,
Then the view imputing existence of self no longer arises.
Through complete cessation of the view imputing a "self,"
The aggregates themselves no longer arise.

4) Analogy: Aggregates Like Mirror, "Self" Like an Unreal Reflected Image

031

It is just as when a person using a polished mirror
Is able to observe the reflection of his own face in it.
This reflection is only something one is able to perceive,
For it has never been something real.

1-032
我见亦如是依阴得显现
如实捡非有犹如镜面影

1-033
如人不执镜不见自面影
如此若析阴我见即不有

1-034
因闻如是义大净命阿难
即得净法眼恒为他说此

1-035
阴执乃至在我见亦恒存
由有我见故业及有恒有

1-036
生死轮三节无初中后转
譬如[3]旋火轮生[4]起互相由

1-037
从自他及二三世不有故
证此我见灭次业报亦然

简体字

1-032
我見亦如是依陰得顯現
如實撿非有猶如鏡面影

1-033
如人不執鏡不見自面影
如此若析陰我見即不有

1-034
因聞如是義大淨命阿難
即得淨法眼恆為他說此

1-035
陰執乃至在我見亦恆存
由有我見故業及有恆有

1-036
生死輪三節無初中後轉
譬如[3]旋火輪生[4]起互相由

1-037
從自他及二三世不有故
證此我見滅次業報亦然

正體字

a) The Aggregates Reflect a False Image of "Self"

032
The view imputing existence of self is just the same.
It is in reliance upon the aggregates that it is able to appear.
Examined in accordance with reality, it is found to be non-existent
Just as in the case of the mirror's reflection of a face.

b) Releasing the Aggregate "Mirror," the "Reflection" of Self Ceases

033
Were a person to refrain from holding up the mirror,
He would no longer observe the reflection of his own face.
So too, when one analytically contemplates the aggregates,
Then the view imputing a self straightaway ceases to exist.

c) Ānanda's Acquisition of the Dharma Eye via This Analogy

034
It was on account of hearing this same concept
That the great *ārya*, Ānanda,
Immediately achieved purification of the Dharma eye
And then repeatedly explained this for the sake of others.

5) Attachment to the Aggregates Ensures Continuation of Cyclic Existence

035
So long as attachment to the aggregates continues to be sustained,
The view imputing a "self" shall be constantly retained as well.
It is based on the presence of a view imputing existence of a self
That "karmic action" and "becoming" continue constantly on.[26]

6) Twirling Firebrand Analogy: Cyclic Existence Is a Continuous Cycle

036
As for the three phases in the wheel of cyclic births and deaths,
As it turns, none are "prior," "intermediary," or "subsequent."
Just as with the "wheel" appearing by the twirling of a firebrand,
Their generation is interdependently caused.[27]

7) Cessation of Self-Imputing View Entails the End of Karma-Bound Action

037
It does not exist having arisen from itself, from some other, or both,
And also does not exist in any of the three periods of time,
Once this is realized, the view imputing a "self" ceases
Along with subsequent karmic actions and retributions.[28]

简体字	正體字
1-038 如此见因果生起及灭尽 故不执实有世间有及无	1-038 如此見因果生起及滅盡 故不執實有世間有及無
1-039 愚人闻此法能尽一切苦 由无智生怖于无怖畏处	1-039 愚人聞此法能盡一切苦 由無智生怖於無怖畏處
1-040 涅盘处无此汝云何生怖 如所说实空云何令汝怖	1-040 涅槃處無此汝云何生怖 如所說實空云何令汝怖
1-041 解脱无我阴汝若[5]受此法 舍我及诸阴汝云何不乐	1-041 解脫無我陰汝若[5]受此法 捨我及諸陰汝云何不樂
1-042 无尚非涅盘何况当是有 有无执净尽佛说名涅盘	1-042 無尚非涅槃何況當是有 有無執淨盡佛說名涅槃
1-043 若略说邪见谓拨无因果 此[6]今非福满恶道因最重	1-043 若略說邪見謂撥無因果 此[6]今非福滿惡道因最重

8) UNDERSTANDING OF ORIGINATION AND CESSATION HALTS EXTREME VIEWS

038
Having perceived cause-and-effect in this manner,
Its arising, and its complete cessation,
One therefore refrains from seizing upon there being any reality
To the world's existence or its non-existence.[29]

9) THE FOOLISH NEEDLESSLY FEAR THIS DHARMA

039
When the foolish hear this Dharma
So able to bring about the ending of all suffering,
Because they have no knowledge of it, they become fearful
Of that station in which one has nothing to fear.[30]

10) SINCE YOU DON'T FEAR A FUTURE NIRVĀṆA, WHY FEAR "EMPTINESS"?

040
That there shall be none of this in the station of nirvāṇa—
How could that generate any fear in you?
As for what we explain as "emptiness of intrinsic reality,"
How could this cause you to be struck with fear?[31]

11) SINCE NON-SELF IS INEVITABLE IN NIRVĀṆA, WHY FEAR IT NOW?

041
On gaining that liberation, there is neither self nor aggregates.
If you do accept this dharma,
Then, how can you be displeased
At the prospect of relinquishing self and aggregates?

12) THE INCOMPATIBILITY OF EXTREME VIEWS AND NIRVĀṆA

042
Not even "non-existence" qualifies as nirvāṇa.
How much the less might "existence" qualify as such?
The complete end of attachments to existence or non-existence—
The Buddha described this as essential to nirvāṇa.

2. DEFINITION OF WRONG VIEW AND ITS DISASTROUS EFFECTS

043
Were one to provide a summary description of "wrong view,"
One would refer to "dismissing cause-and-effect as non-existent."
This causes one to become filled with non-meritorious karma
And is the weightiest cause for entering the wretched destinies.[32]

简体字	正體字
1-044 若略说正见谓[7]信有因果 能令福德满善道因最上	1-044 若略說正見謂[7]信有因果 能令福德滿善道因最上
1-045 由智有无寂超度福非福 故离善恶道佛说名解脱	1-045 由智有無寂超度福非福 故離善惡道佛說名解脫
1-046 若见生有因智人舍无执 由见灭共因是故舍有执	1-046 若見生有因智人捨無執 由見滅共因是故捨有執
1-047 先俱生二因实义则非因 假名无依故及生非实故	1-047 先俱生二因實義則非因 假名無依故及生非實故
1-048 若此有彼有譬如长及短 由此生彼生譬如灯与光	1-048 若此有彼有譬如長及短 由此生彼生譬如燈與光
1-049 先长后为短不然非性故 光明不生故灯亦非实有	1-049 先長後為短不然非性故 光明不生故燈亦非實有

3. Definition of Right View and Its Auspicious Effects

044

Were one to provide a summary description of "right view,"
One would refer to "believing in the existence of cause-and-effect."
This is able to cause one to gain a full measure of merit
And is the most superior cause for rebirth in the good destinies.[33]

4. Wisdom's Preeminence Over Dualities and Its Generation of Liberation

045

Through wisdom, "existence" versus "non-existence" is stilled,
One steps beyond [ideas about] "merit" versus "non-merit,"
And one transcends [concern over] "good" versus "bad" destinies.
The Buddha described this as tantamount to gaining liberation.[34]

a. The Wise Relinquish Attachment to Asserting Non-existence or Existence

046

Having perceived that production has causes,
The wise relinquish any attachment to "non-existence."
Through perceiving that cessation involves joint causation,
One thereby relinquishes any attachment to "existence."[35]

b. The Unreality of Production and Both Prior and Concurrent Cause

047

As for two types of causation, prior cause and concurrent cause,
According to [ultimate] reality, they do not qualify as causes.
This is because artificial designations are devoid of any bases,
And is also because "production" itself does not qualify as real.[36]

c. The Fallaciousness of Polarity and Interdependency-Based Designations

048

Where the existence of "that" is linked to the existence of "this,"
As with "long" and "short"—
And where, because "this" is produced, "that" is produced,
As with a "lantern" and "light"—[these are inadmissible].

049

Where there is first something "long" and later something "short,"
This is invalid, for these [attributes] are not intrinsic to their nature.
Because, when it is not producing light,
The "lantern" itself is not genuinely existent.[37]

简体字	正體字
1-050 如此因果生若见不执无 已信世真实由乱心所生	1-050 如此因果生若見不執無 已信世真實由亂心所生
1-051 见灭非虚故即证得真如 是故不执有不依二解脱	1-051 見滅非虛故即證得真如 是故不執有不依二解脫
1-052 色是远所见若近最分明 鹿渴若实[8]已色云何近不见	1-052 色是遠所見若近最分明 鹿渴若實[8]已色云何近不見
1-053 若远于实智即见世间有 证实则不见无相如鹿渴	1-053 若遠於實智即見世間有 證實則不見無相如鹿渴
1-054 如鹿渴似水非水非实物 如此阴似人非人非实法	1-054 如鹿渴似水非水非實物 如此陰似人非人非實法
1-055 计鹿渴为水往彼若饮此 若无执为水如此人愚痴	1-055 計鹿渴為水往彼若飲此 若無執為水如此人愚癡

Chapter 1: *On Gaining Happiness and Liberation*

d. CONDITIONED ARISING COUNTERS NIHILISM; REALISM'S ROOTS IN DELUSION
050
If one [rightly] perceives such cases of cause-and-effect production,
He does not seize on [the nihilist view asserting] "non-existence."
Where one has believed in the actual reality of the world,
That is a product of a mind that is confused.[38]

e. REALIZATION OF TRUE SUCHNESS, NON-ATTACHMENT, AND NON-DUAL LIBERATION
051
Through perceiving that "cessation" is not a false notion,
One straightaway gains realization of true suchness.
One therefore desists from attachment to "existence,"
Refrains from relying on dualities, and gains liberation.

5. MIRAGE ANALOGY FOR THE WORLD, SELF, AGGREGATES, AND DHARMAS
a. PERCEPTIBILITY OF FORMS CONTRASTED WITH IMPERCEPTIBILITY OF A MIRAGE
052
Forms are such that, one may observe them from a distance,
And then, on coming closer, they appear with distinct detail.
If the forms in a mirage were real,[39]
Why does one fail to see them at all on drawing up close?[40]

b. THE UNREALITY OF THE WORLD
053
If one abides far away from genuine wisdom,
One straightaway views the world as existing.
On gaining realization of reality, one no longer perceives this.
It is then found to be signless, just like a mirage.

c. REFUTATION OF THE REALITY OF THE FIVE AGGREGATES
054
Just as a mirage has the appearance of water,
But is not water, and is not a real entity—
In this same fashion, the aggregates appear to be a person,
But are not a person, and are not real dharmas.

d. CLINGING TO ILLUSION AS INDICATIVE OF FOOLISHNESS
055
Having determined that a mirage consists of water,
One might reasonably go toward it, intending to drink from it.
If, discovering it to be non-existent, one still clings to it as "water"—
This sort of person would be deemed to be a fool.

1-056
世间如鹿渴若执实有无
此即是无明痴故无解脱

1-057
执无堕恶趣执有生善道
若能知如实不二依解脱

1-058
不乐有无执由择真实义
若堕于无执何不说堕有

1-059
若言由破有义至故堕无
如此破无故云何不堕有

1-060
无言行及心由依菩提故
若说彼堕无何因不堕有

1-061
僧佉鞞世师尼揵说人阴
约世汝问彼若说过有无

1-062
是不可言法以过有无故
汝应知甚深佛正教甘露

简体字

1-056
世間如鹿渴若執實有無
此即是無明癡故無解脫

1-057
執無墮惡趣執有生善道
若能知如實不二依解脫

1-058
不樂有無執由擇真實義
若墮於無執何不說墮有

1-059
若言由破有義至故墮無
如此破無故云何不墮有

1-060
無言行及心由依菩提故
若說彼墮無何因不墮有

1-061
僧佉鞞世師尼揵說人陰
約世汝問彼若說過有無

1-062
是不可言法以過有無故
汝應知甚深佛正教甘露

正體字

Chapter 1: *On Gaining Happiness and Liberation*   49

    e. CLINGING TO REALITY OF THE WORLD IS FOOLISH AND PREVENTS LIBERATION

056
The world is comparable to a mirage.
If one seizes on it as being truly existent or non-existent,
This is just ignorance.
It is due to delusion that one remains without liberation.

    6. POLAR ATTACHMENTS BEGET SAṂSĀRA; REALITY COGNITION BEGETS LIBERATION

057
By seizing on "non-existence," one may fall to the wretched destinies.
By seizing on "existence," one may be reborn in the good destinies.
If one is able to know things in accordance with reality,
One gains the liberation not reliant on dualities.[41]

    a. REFUTATION: DISINCLINATION TO ATTACHMENT DOES NOT ENTAIL NIHILISM

058
Disinclination to seize on [views asserting] existence or non-existence
Originates with discernment of the meaning of reality.
If [one claims this entails] falling into a "non-existence" attachment,
Why not [also] claim this entails falling into "existence" attachment?[42]

059
If one claims that, by refuting [views validating] "existence,"
One falls by force of logic into implicitly validating "non-existence,"
Then, following this same logic, by refuting "non-existence,"
Why wouldn't one fall into implicitly validating "existence"?[43]

060
This non-validation of words, actions, or thoughts [as ultimately real]
Is a result of reliance on bodhi.
If one claims this entails an implicit fall into validating non-existence,
Why would that not also entail a fall into validating existence?[44]

    7. THE UNIQUENESS OF BUDDHISM'S TRANSCENDENCE OF DUAL CONCEPTS

061
As for the Sāṃkhyas, the Vaiśeṣikas,
The Nirgranthas, those who assert aggregate-based personhood,
And the worldly traditions—you should interrogate them all
As to whether their claims transcend existence and non-existence.[45]

062
As for this ineffable Dharma,
Because it transcends both "existence" and "non-existence,"
You should realize it is the extremely profound
Sweet-dew ambrosia (*amṛta*) of the Buddha's orthodox teaching.

简体字	正體字
1-063 如晓无去来亦无一念住 若体过三世何世为实有	**1-063** 如曉無去來亦無一念住 若體過三世何世為實有
1-064 二世无去来现在实不住 [lokanirvāṇayos tasmād viśeṣaḥ ka ivārthataḥ] (64c-d emended via Sanskrit.)	**1-064** 二世無去來現在實不住 [lokanirvāṇayos tasmād viśeṣaḥ ka ivārthataḥ] (64c-d emended via Sanskrit.)
1-065 [sthiter abhāvād udayo nirodhaś ca na tattvataḥ] (65a-b emended via Sanskrit.) 世生及住灭此言云何实	**1-065** [sthiter abhāvād udayo nirodhaś ca na tattvataḥ] (65a-b emended via Sanskrit.) 世生及住滅此言云何實
1-066 若恒有变异何法不念灭 若无念念灭云何有变异	**1-066** 若恒有變異何法不念滅 若無念念滅云何有變異
1-067 若言念念灭分具分灭故 不等证见故此二无道理	**1-067** 若言念念滅分具分滅故 不等證見故此二無道理
1-068 若念灭皆尽云何有故物 若坚无念灭故物云何成	**1-068** 若念滅皆盡云何有故物 若堅無念滅故物云何成
1-069 如刹那后际前中际亦有 由刹那三分故世念无住	**1-069** 如剎那後際前中際亦有 由剎那三分故世念無住

8. Unreality of Three Times and Three Marks (Arising, Abiding, Destruction)

063
If one understands [the world] has no going thither [into the past],
No coming hither [from the future], no abiding for even an instant—
If its essential nature transcends even the three periods of time—
What world might one then claim possesses any real existence?[46]

064
The two times, [past and future], involve no going or coming,
And, in reality, there is no abiding in the present,
[*lokanirvāṇayos tasmād viśeṣaḥ ka ivārthataḥ*]: (64c-d via Sanskrit.)
[How could it be then that the world and nirvāṇa
Possess any differences which are real?][47]

065
[*sthiter abhāvād udayo nirodhaś ca na tattvataḥ*]: (65a-b via Sanskrit.)
[Since "abiding" doesn't exist,
"Production" and "cessation" are also not real.]
As for the world's "production," its "abiding," and its "cessation,"
How could such designations correspond to reality?[48]

9. On Constant Instant-by-Instant Destruction and Change

066
If there is a constantly occurring process of change,
What dharma would not undergo instant-by-instant destruction?
If no instant-by-instant destruction occurred,
How could there exist any process of change?

067
If one asserts that instant-by-instant destruction
Is by partial destruction in either parts or the whole—
Because they involve views validating inconsistencies,
These two theories are groundless.

068
If instant-by-instant destruction involved cessation of the whole,
How could any "old" things ever exist?
And if there were absolutely no instant-by-instant destruction,
How then could old things become so?

10. Deconstruction of Instants and Refutation of the World's Abiding

069
If the end of a *kṣaṇa*[49] (an instant) exists,
Then the beginning and middle exist as well.
Because of the three components of a *kṣaṇa*,
There is no abiding of the world even for an instant.

1-070 是一念三际应择际如念 前中后三际不由自他成 1-071 非一[9]念分故若无分何有 离一多云何离有何法无 1-072 由灭及对治若言有成无 此无及对治何法有无故 1-073 是故世涅盘由义不成有 世间有后际他问佛默然 1-074 是尊一切智故[1]智人识佛 由此甚深法不说非器处 1-075 如此解脱法甚深无系摄 诸佛一切智故说无依底	1-070 是一念三際應擇際如念 前中後三際不由自他成 1-071 非一[9]念分故若無分何有 離一多云何離有何法無 1-072 由滅及對治若言有成無 此無及對治何法有無故 1-073 是故世涅槃由義不成有 世間有後際他問佛默然 1-074 是尊一切智故[1]智人識佛 由此甚深法不說非器處 1-075 如此解脫法甚深無繫攝 諸佛一切智故說無依底
简体字	正體字

070
As for the three component phases of this single instant,
One should analyze each such phase just as one does the instant.
As for those three phases, beginning, middle, and end,
They are neither self-created nor other-created.

11. Deconstruction of Unitary Entities; Dependence of Dual Designations
071
Because they have parts, instants are not unitary entities.
If they do not exist as such, how could any parts exist?
Without the "singular," how could there be the "many"?
Without "existence," what dharma could be "non-existent"?

12. As "Existence" Is a Fallacy, How Could any Entity Be "Non-existent"?
072
If one claims that, either through destruction or counteraction,
Something which exists may become non-existent—
As for this "non-existence" [by destruction] or "counteraction,"
What dharma's "existence" might thence become "non-existent"?[50]

13. Recondite Dharma and the Common Person's Misapprehension of It.
a. Non-existence of the World and Nirvāṇa and the Buddha's Silence
073
Therefore, since the world and nirvāṇa
Are not establishable through reason as "existing,"
When the question, "Does the world have an end point?"
Was asked of him by others, the Buddha simply remained silent.[51]

b. Recondite Dharmas Were Not Discussed with Those Unfit
074
This was to preserve respect for [the ineffability of] omniscience.
Hence the wise recognize that the Buddha,
Because this is an extremely recondite dharma,
Wouldn't speak of it to those with no capacity to comprehend it.[52]

c. The Absence of Dependencies in Buddha's Profound Dharmas
075
Dharmas connected with liberation such as these
Are extremely profound and unsubsumed by any other.
Because the Buddhas are omniscient,
Their discourse is free of any dependent bases.

简体字	正體字
1-076 于无依着法过有无二边 世人受依着由痴惊怖失	1-076 於無依著法過有無二邊 世人受依著由癡驚怖失
1-077 彼自失坏他怖畏无依处 王愿汝不动莫由彼自坏	1-077 彼自失壞他怖畏無依處 王願汝不動莫由彼自壞
1-078 为汝成不坏我当说真理 由依无倒合离有无二执	1-078 為汝成不壞我當說真理 由依無倒合離有無二執
1-079 此过福非福甚深义明了 非身见怖空二人境当说	1-079 此過福非福甚深義明了 非身見怖空二人境當說
1-080 四大及空识一聚俱非人 若合离非人云何执人有	1-080 四大及空識一聚俱非人 若合離非人云何執人有
1-081 如六界非人聚故虚非实 一一界同然由聚故非实	1-081 如六界非人聚故虛非實 一一界同然由聚故非實

d. The Worldly, Frightened by Transcendent Dharma, Fall to Ruin

076
Faced with this Dharma free of dependencies or attachments
And beyond the two extremes, "existence" and "non-existence,"
People of the world, subscribing to dependencies and attachments,
Due to delusion, are frightened by it, and thereby come to ruin.

e. Having Met Ruin Themselves, Be Warned: They Visit Ruin on Others

077
Having wrought their own destruction, they bring ruin on others,
Causing them to be frightened of what is free of dependent bases.
One prays, O King, that you will remain unmoved,
You mustn't bring ruin on yourself through the influence of others.

f. Through Truth, One Avoids Inverted Views and Attachments

078
That you may become invulnerable to ruin,
I shall proceed to explain what is true.
By relying on this, one avoids involvement in inverted views
And abandons two attachments, "existence" and "non-existence."[53]

g. This Teaching is Profound, Unsuited for Those Clinging to the Superficial

079
This goes beyond both merit and non-merit,[54]
And embodies the extremely profound meaning with utter clarity.
As for persons viewing body as self or fear-struck by emptiness—
It is not such as should be explained in the vicinity of those two.[55]

14. Refutation of Inherent Existence in the Six Elements

080
The four primary elements along with space and consciousness,
Whether alone or aggregated, don't qualify as a "person."
If, either united or separate, they don't qualify as a "person,"
How could one seize upon the existence of a "person" in them?[56]

081
Just as these six elements together do not qualify as a person
Because, being a mere assemblage, they are false and not real,
So too, each and every element, on its own, is just the same:
Because each is a mere assemblage, it does not qualify as real.

简体字	正體字
1–082 阴非我我所离阴我不显 不如薪火杂何依阴成我	1–082 陰非我我所離陰我不顯 不如薪火雜何依陰成我
1–083 地界非三大地中亦无三 三中亦无地相离互不成	1–083 地界非三大地中亦無三 三中亦無地相離互不成
1–084 地水火风大各自性不成 一离三不成三离一亦尔	1–084 地水火風大各自性不成 一離三不成三離一亦爾
1–085 一三及三一相离若不成 各各自不成彼相离云何	1–085 一三及三一相離若不成 各各自不成彼相離云何
1–086 若各离自成离薪何无火 动碍及相聚水风地亦然	1–086 若各離自成離薪何無火 動礙及相聚水風地亦然
1–087 若火[2]不自成三云何各立 三大缘生义相违云何成	1–087 若火[2]不自成三云何各立 三大緣生義相違云何成
1–088 若彼各自成云何更互有 若各自不成云何互成有	1–088 若彼各自成云何更互有 若各自不成云何互成有
1–089 若言不相离诸大各自成 不[3]杂则不共若*杂非独成	1–089 若言不相離諸大各自成 不[3]雜則不共若*雜非獨成

a. DISMISSAL OF THE AGGREGATES AS CONSTITUTING A SELF
082
The aggregates do not qualify as a self or as possessions of a self.
Apart from the aggregates, a "self" does not appear.
Because they are not mixed in the manner of fuel and fire,[57]
On what basis then could the aggregates constitute a self?
083
The earth element isn't the same as any of the three other elements,
Nor do any of those three exist within the earth element,
Nor does the earth element exist within any of those three.
Nor [is their existence] establishable either separately or mutually.
084
Each of the primary elements of earth, water, fire, and wind
Is not established as possessing its own inherently existing nature.
Just as any one is not establishable separate from the other three,
So too is this the case for any three when separated from any one.
085
If any one relative to the other three and three relative to any one
Can't be established [as existing] when separated from others,
And each can't be established [as inherently existent] on its own,
How could that one even be separated from the others in any case?
086
If each could be independently established when separated,
Why is there no burning once fire is separated from its fuel?
As for [the qualities of] motility, obstruction, and cohesion,
They depend on water, wind, and earth in the same manner.
087
Since fire cannot be established on its own,
How could any of the other three stand on their own either?
As three elements serve the principle of production via conditions,
On what basis might one prove incompatiblity with this in the other?
088
If they each could be established as independently existent,
How could they each additionally exist interdependently?
Also, if each cannot be established as independently existent,
How could it serve a role in mutually-established existence either?
089
Were one to claim they do not abide separately from each other,
Even as each element's existence is independently established—
If they are not interrelated, then they have no conjoint existence.
And if they are interrelated, isolated existence can't be established.

简体字	正體字
1-090 诸大非各成云何各性相 各成无偏多故相假名说	1-090 諸大非各成云何各性相 各成無偏多故相假名說
1-091 色声香味触简择义如大 眼色识无明业生择亦尔	1-091 色聲香味觸簡擇義如大 眼色識無明業生擇亦爾
1-092 作者业及事数合因果世 短长及名想非想择亦然	1-092 作者業及事數合因果世 短長及名想非想擇亦然
1-093 地水风火等长短及小大 善恶言识智智中灭无馀	1-093 地水風火等長短及小大 善惡言識智智中滅無餘
1-094 如识处无形无边遍一切 此中地等大一切皆灭尽	1-094 如識處無形無邊遍一切 此中地等大一切皆滅盡
1-095 于此无相智短长善恶[4]业 名色[5]及诸阴如此灭无馀	1-095 於此無相智短長善惡[4]業 名色[5]及諸陰如此滅無餘

090

If the existence of each element is not independently established,
How could each possess its own inherent characteristics?
If independently established, they can't manifest predominance.⁵⁸
Therefore their "characteristics" are mere artificial designations.

> 15. ANALYSIS OF THE 6 SENSE OBJECTS, 18 REALMS, AND 12-FOLD CAUSAL CHAIN IS SIMILAR

091

As for visible forms, sounds, smells, tastes, and touchables,
The principles are analyzed in the same manner as the elements.
Also: eye, form, consciousness, [eighteen sense realms], ignorance,
Action, birth, [the twelve causal links]—their analysis is the same.⁵⁹

> 16. SO TOO THE AGENT OF ACTIONS, KARMA, PHENOMENA, NUMBERS, CONJUNCTION, CAUSE, EFFECT, TIME, SHORT AND LONG, DESIGNATIONS, THOUGHT, ETC.

092

The agent of actions, karmic action, and objective phenomena—
Numbers, conjunction, cause, effect, and the periods of time—
Short and long, as well as naming, perceptive thought,
And non-perception—they should be analyzed in the same way.

> 17. WISDOM DEMOLISHES THE ELEMENTS, DUALITIES, GOOD, EVIL, WORDS, CONSCIOUSNESS, KNOWLEDGE

093

Earth, water, wind, fire, and so forth—
Long and short as well as small and large—
Good, evil, words, consciousness, and knowledge—
They are so demolished by wisdom that no trace remains.

> a. LIKE THE STATION OF BOUNDLESS CONSCIOUSNESS, THIS WISDOM EXTENDS EVERYWHERE, DEMOLISHING EVERYTHING

094

Just as no forms exist in the station of boundless consciousness,
And just as it is boundless and universally pervasive,
So too in this [wisdom]: Earth and the other primary elements
Are all brought to complete destruction.

095

In this wisdom cognizing signlessness,
Short and long, good and evil, karmic actions,
Name-and-form, and also the aggregates—
As with these others, they are so demolished as to leave no trace.

简体字	正體字
1-096 如此等于识由无明先有 于识若起智此等后皆尽	1-096 如此等於識由無明先有 於識若起智此等後皆盡
1-097 如是等世法是然识火薪 由实量火光世识薪烧尽	1-097 如是等世法是然識火薪 由實量火光世識薪燒盡
1-098 由痴别有无后简择真如 寻有既不得无云何可得	1-098 由癡別有無後簡擇真如 尋有既不得無云何可得
1-099 由无色所成故空但名字 离大何为色故色亦唯名	1-099 由無色所成故空但名字 離大何為色故色亦唯名
1-100 受想行及识应思如四大 四大如我虚六界非人法	1-100 受想行及識應思如四大 四大如我虛六界非人法

096
Phenomena such as these manifest to consciousness
Due to the prior existence of "ignorance."
If one brings wisdom to bear in one's consciousness,
All such [delusion-based perceptions] are finally caused to cease.[60]

097
Dharmas of the world such as these
Are fuel for a fire burning up [deluded] consciousness.
Producing a fiery illumination able to fathom reality,
The fuel of worldly consciousness is entirely burned up.

098
Due to delusion, one discriminated existence versus non-existence,
Yet subsequently may be able to skillfully discern true suchness.
Since, even searching for bases of existence, one can't find them,
How then could "non-existence" be amenable to apprehension?

099
Because it is established only through an absence of form,
"Space" is therefore but a mere designation.
Apart from the primary elements, of what might "form" consist?
Therefore the form aggregate too is but a mere designation.

100
Feeling, perception, karmic formative factors, and consciousness
Should be contemplated in the same way as the four elements.
The four elements, as in the case of the "self," are false concepts.
The six elements don't qualify as dharmas constituting a "person."

[6] 宝行王正论

杂品第二

2-001
如分分[7]拆蕉无馀尽不有
约六界[8]拆人尽空亦如是

2-002
是故佛正说一切法无我
但六界名法决判实无我

2-003
我无我二义如实捡不得
是故如来遮我无我二边

2-004
见闻觉知言佛说无实虚
二相待成故此二如实无

2-005
如实捡世间过实亦过虚
则世间依实故堕于有无

Chapter Two
Advice on Various Topics

II. Chapter 2: Advice on Various Topics
  A. Analogy: The "Person" is as Insubstantial as the Plantain
001
Just as when, part-by-part, one pulls apart a plantain plant
So that it utterly ceases to exist, leaving no trace,
When, according to the six elements, one takes apart a "person,"
It too is found to be entirely empty in just this same manner.

  B. The Buddha Declared the Absence of any Inherent Existence in Dharmas
002
Thus it is that the Buddha rightly proclaimed
That all dharmas are devoid of any "self."
There is only a dharma of naming referencing the six elements.
One may judge with certainty that, in reality, there is no "self."

    1. The Buddha Disallowed Both Existence and Non-existence of "Self"
003
As for the two concepts of "self" and "non-existence of self,"
If analyzed in accord with reality, they cannot be apprehended.
It is for this reason that the Tathāgata excluded
The two extremes of "self" and "non-existence of self."

    2. So Too in the Case of Duality-Based Designations
004
As for statements based on knowing via seeing, hearing, [et cetera],[61]
The Buddha stated that they are not inherently either true or false.
Because they are products of interdependent duality,
Such dual [concepts] have no reality-based [intrinsic] existence.

005
When one contemplates the world in terms of ultimate reality,
It transcends the "true" even while transcending the "false."
Hence, from a reality-based standpoint, the world's perspective
Falls into the fallacy of reifying both existence and non-existence.

简体字	正體字
2-006 若法遍不如云何佛得说 有边及无边有二与无二	2-006 若法遍不如云何佛得說 有邊及無邊有二與無二
2-007 过去佛无量现来过算数 过数众生边三世由佛显	2-007 過去佛無量現來過算數 過數眾生邊三世由佛顯
2-008 世间无长因此际约世显 世间过有无云何佛记边	2-008 世間無長因此際約世顯 世間過有無云何佛記邊
2-009 由法如此深于凡秘不说 说世如幻化是佛甘露教	2-009 由法如此深於凡祕不說 說世如幻化是佛甘露教
2-010 譬如幻化像/象生灭尚可见 此9像/象及生灭实义捡非有	2-010 譬如幻化像/象生滅尚可見 此9像/象及生滅實義撿非有
2-011 世间如幻化生灭可见尔 世间及生灭[10]约实义皆虚	2-011 世間如幻化生滅可見爾 世間及生滅[10]約實義皆虛
2-012 幻像/象无从来去亦无有处 但迷众生心由实有不住	2-012 幻像/象無從來去亦無有處 但迷眾生心由實有不住

3. The Rationale for the Buddha's Remaining Silent

006
Where all dharmas at issue universally fail to accord [with reality],
How could the Buddha have been able to affirm
Boundedness, unboundedness,
Both, or neither, [*et cetera*]?[62]

4. Challenge: The Buddha Erred in Declaring Beings Boundlessly Many

007 [Challenge]:
Past buddhas have been incalculably many.
Those of the present and the future surpass enumeration.
That they would surpass the limited number of beings
Across the three times was made obvious by the Buddha.[63]

008
The world is free of any causes for increase [in beings].
The limits to this become apparent as a stricture imposed by time.
[Yet you say:] "As the world transcends existence and non-existence,
How could Buddha make definitive assertions on boundedness?"

5. Response: Not So. The World Is Illusory, Transcends Dual Concepts, etc.

009 [Response (9a–15d)]:
Because this Dharma is so profound,
When with the common person, it is kept secret and not discussed.
The teaching that the world is like an illusory conjuration
Is the sweet-dew ambrosia (*amṛta*) of the Buddha's teaching.

010
This is comparable to a magically-conjured elephant[64]
Which, even being such, may be seen to appear and disappear.
As for this elephant as well as its appearance and disappearance,
From the perspective of reality, it is discerned to be non-existent.

011
The world too is like an illusory conjuration.
The perceptibility of its production and destruction is also just so.
The world as well as its production and destruction,
From the perspective of reality, is in every case false.

012
A magically-conjured elephant has no place from which it comes.[65]
When it goes, it has no continued residing anywhere, either.
It serves only to delude the minds of beings.
In reality, its "existence" involves no abiding at all.

2-013 (Emendation via Sanskrit Text)
[*Tathā māyopamo loko naiti yāti na kutracit* |
cittamohanamātratvād bhāvatvena na tiṣṭhati ‖]

2-014
世體過三世若爾世何實
[11]誰言說有無有無實無義

2-015
故佛約四句不記說世間
由有無皆虛此虛不虛故

2-016
是身不淨相麁證智境界
恒數數所見尚不入心[1]住

2-017
況正法微細甚深無依底
難證於散心云何可易入

2-018
故佛初成道捨[2]說欲涅槃
由見此正法甚深故難解

2-019
若法非正了即害不聰人
由不如執此墮邪見穢坑

013 (Emendation via Sanskrit Text)
[*Tathā māyopamo loko naiti yāti na kutracit* |
cittamohanamātratvād bhāvatvena na tiṣṭhati‖]
[Even so, the world is like a magical conjuration
Which comes from nowhere and goes to nowhere.
It merely serves to delude the mind,
For its "existence" involves no abiding at all.]⁶⁶

014
The essential nature of the world transcends even the three times.
If so, what reality could there be to the world?
Apart from mere statements about existence versus non-existence,⁶⁷
In reality, "existent" and "non-existent" have no intrinsic meaning.

015
Hence Buddha, when compelled to speak in terms of the tetralemma,
Declined to make definitive statements regarding the world.⁶⁸
Since "existence" versus "non-existence" polarities are all false,
This [silence as a response to] fallaciousness was not itself fallacious.⁶⁹

    C. As obvious Teachings Aren't Easily Absorbed, It's Truer Yet of Subtleties

016
This body's characteristic of being impure
Is a mind state known even at coarse levels of realization.
Though constantly and repeatedly observed,
It may yet fail to enter and abide in the mind.

017
How much the more might this be so for right Dharma's subtleties,
Being so extremely recondite and free of dependent bases?
Given they are difficult to realize with a scattered mind,
How could it be that they might easily enter?

    D. Hence the Buddha Initially Refrained from Proclaiming the Dharma

018
Therefore the Buddha, on first gaining realization of the Path,
Refrained from proclaiming it and was about to enter nirvāṇa.
This was because he perceived that this right Dharma,
Due to its extreme profundity, is difficult to comprehend.

    E. Misunderstanding Dharma May Even Lead to One's Downfall

019
In a case where the Dharma is understood incorrectly,
It may bring immediate harm to those not acutely intelligent.
Thus, by seizing on it in a manner not according [with its intent],
They may fall into a pit of defilement by wrong views.

简体字	正體字
2-020 人识法不明由自高轻法 起谤坏自身下首堕地狱	2-020 人識法不明由自高輕法 起謗壞自身下首墮地獄
2-021 譬如胜饮食偏用遭危害 若如理量食得寿力强乐	2-021 譬如勝飲食偏用遭危害 若如理量食得壽力強樂
2-022 若偏解正法遭苦亦如此 若能如理解感乐及菩提	2-022 若偏解正法遭苦亦如此 若能如理解感樂及菩提
2-023 智人于正法舍谤及邪[3]执 于正智起用故成如意事	2-023 智人於正法捨謗及邪[3]執 於正智起用故成如意事
2-024 由不了此法人起长我见 因此造三业次生善恶道	2-024 由不了此法人起長我見 因此造三業次生善惡道
2-025 乃至未证法能除灭我见 恒敬起正勤于戒施忍等	2-025 乃至未證法能除滅我見 恒敬起正勤於戒施忍等
2-026 作事法为先及法为中后 谓无虚真理现来[4]汝不沈	2-026 作事法為先及法為中後 謂無虛真理現來[4]汝不沈

020

If a person's awareness of Dharma lacks clear comprehension,
Through elevating himself and taking the Dharma lightly,
He may initiate slanders, bring ruin on himself,
And plummet headfirst down into the hells.

> 1. ANALOGY: AS IN THE RIGHT OR WRONG USE OF SUPERIOR FOOD AND DRINK

021

This is analogous to [gaining access to] superior drink and food.
If one is extreme in consuming it, he encounters perilous harm.
If, however, if he is reasonably measured in his eating,
He gains long life, strength, health, and happiness.

022

If one is skewed in the way he understands right Dharma,
He encounters suffering in just this same way.
If, however, he is able to accord with reason in understanding it,
He brings on both happiness and bodhi as a result.

> F. THE WISE AVOID SLANDER OF RIGHT DHARMA AND WRONG ATTACHMENTS

023

With respect to right Dharma, the wise person
Avoids both slander and erroneous attachments.
With respect to right knowledge, he brings it forth in a useful way.
He thus succeeds in creating circumstances according to his wishes.

> G. FAILING TO UNDERSTAND THIS DHARMA PERPETUATES CYCLIC EXISTENCE

024

On account of failing to completely understand this Dharma,
People generate and increase the view imputing existence of "self."
On account of this, they create the three types of karmic actions[70]
And consequently take birth in both good and bad destinies.

> H. DIRECT INSTRUCTIONS TO THE KING
> 1. ONE MUST PERSEVERE IN THE PERFECTIONS

025

So long as one has not yet gained realization of this Dharma,
Able to demolish the view imputing existence of "self,"
One should be constantly reverential and generate right effort
In the practice of moral virtue, giving, patience, and the rest.[71]

> 2. THE DHARMA SHOULD BE ONE'S PRIORITY IN THE BEGINNING, MIDDLE, AND END

026

Where, in the carrying out of works, Dharma comes "first,"
Even to the point that Dharma also comes "middle" and "last,"
It is said that, staying free of falseness and reliant on true principle,
You will avoid sinking away in the present and future.

2-027
因法现好名乐临死无怖
来生受富乐故应恒事法

2-028
唯法是正治因法天下爱
若[5]主感民爱现来不被诳

2-029
若非法治化主遭臣厌恶
由世间[6]憎恶现来不欢喜

2-030
王法欺诳他是大难恶道
恶智邪[7]命论云何说为正

2-031
若人专诳他云何说正事
因此于万生恒遭他欺诳

2-032
若欲使怨忧舍失取其[8]德
己利由此圆即令怨忧恼

2-033
约施及爱语利行与同利
愿汝摄世间因此弘正法

简体字

2-027
因法現好名樂臨死無怖
來生受富樂故應恒事法

2-028
唯法是正治因法天下愛
若[5]主感民愛現來不被諕

2-029
若非法治化主遭臣厭惡
由世間[6]憎惡現來不歡喜

2-030
王法欺諕他是大難惡道
惡智邪[7]命論云何說為正

2-031
若人專諕他云何說正事
因此於萬生恒遭他欺諕

2-032
若欲使怨憂捨失取其[8]德
己利由此圓即令怨憂惱

2-033
約施及愛語利行與同利
願汝攝世間因此弘正法

正體字

a. Dharma Ensures Reputation, Happiness, Fearlessness, and Future Felicity

027
Because of Dharma, in this present life, one gains a fine reputation,
One enjoys happiness, and one is free of fear when nearing death.
Then, in future lives, one gains both wealth and happiness.
One should therefore be constant in one's service to the Dharma.

3. Dharma is the Essence of Right and Successful Governance

028
It is only through Dharma that there is right governance.
It is because of the Dharma that the country expresses its affection.
If the ruler inspires the love of the people,
In both present and future, he will not be deceived.

4. Actions Contrary to Dharma Are Wrong Governance and Beget Disaster

029
If he governs in a manner contrary to Dharma,
The ruler encounters disgust and abhorrence in his officials.
Because the world is moved to detest and abhor him,
He finds no cause for joy in either the present or the future.

030
Where royal policy involves cheating and deceiving others,
This evokes great difficulties as well as the wretched destinies.
Where doctrine promotes evil intelligence and wrong livelihood,
How could one assert that this is right?

031
Where a person is devoted to the deception of others,
How could this be described as right endeavor?
Because of this, for a myriad lifetimes,
He will constantly encounter cheating and deception by others.

5. Relinquishing of Faults and Emulation of Goodness Distress Adversaries

032
If one desires to cause distress among one's adversaries,
One need only abandon one's faults and adopt their good qualities.
It is through this means that one perfects one's own benefit
And straightaway causes distress and affliction in adversaries.

6. Use Four Means of Attraction to Draw Followers and Spread Dharma

033
Take up giving, pleasing words,
Beneficial actions, and salutary joint endeavors.[72]
I pray that you will draw in the people of the world
And that, based on this, you will propagate right Dharma.

2-034
王若一实语如生民坚信
此如尊妄语不起他安[9]信

2-035
实意起无违流靡能利他
是说名实语翻此为妄言

2-036
一舍财若明如能隐王失
如此主悋贿能害王众德

2-037
若王[10]静诸恶德深人爱重
因此教明王故应事寂静

2-038
由智王难动自了不信他
永不遭欺诳故决应修智

2-039
依谛舍静智王则具四善
如四德正法人天所赞叹

简体字

2-034
王若一實語如生民堅信
此如尊妄語不起他安[9]信

2-035
實意起無違流靡能利他
是說名實語翻此為妄言

2-036
一捨財若明如能隱王失
如此主悋賄能害王眾德

2-037
若王[10]靜諸惡德深人愛重
因此教明王故應事寂靜

2-038
由智王難動自了不信他
永不遭欺誑故決應修智

2-039
依諦捨靜智王則具四善
如四德正法人天所讚歎

正體字

Chapter 2: *Advice on Various Topics*

7. THE FOUR FOUNDATIONS OF MERITORIOUS QUALITIES
a. THE KING SHOULD REALIZE "TRUTH" GENERATES TRUST; LIES DIMINISH IT

034
When a king utters a single truthful discourse,
It is the same as building in the people a solid trust in him.
By the same token, when he esteems the telling of lies,
He fails to produce in others any confident trust in himself.

035
The power of sincere intentions to create an absence of opposition
Is constrained by the extent to which they may benefit others.[73]
It is this sort of discourse which defines truthfulness.
Whatever stands in opposition to this amounts to false speech.

b. "RELINQUISHMENT" COUNTERS ROYAL FAULTS; MISERLINESS DAMAGES VIRTUE

036
A single act of relinquishing wealth, if done with shining clarity,
Is as if able to place a sovereign's faults in the shade.
In the same way, if a ruler is prone to miserliness or graft,
This is able to inflict damage on a king's manifold virtues.

c. CULTIVATION OF "STILLNESS" ELICITS ESTEEM; A BRILLIANT KING GOVERNS FROM DEEP SERENITY

037
If a king employs stillness in dealing with every sort of evil,
His virtue being profound, he is loved and esteemed by the people.
Because of this, the sovereign made brilliant by the teachings
Responds to present circumstances from the midst of stillness.[74]

d. "WISDOM" MAKES THE KING IMMOVABLE, INDEPENDENT, AND UNDECEIVABLE

038
On account of wisdom, the king may become unshakable.
By comprehending matters himself, he need not trust in others.
In order that he might never encounter cheating and deception,
He most certainly should pursue cultivation of wisdom.

e. THESE FOUR BASES OF MERITORIOUS QUALITIES ENGENDER GOODNESS AND PRAISE

039
If he relies on truth, relinquishing, stillness, and wisdom,
A king thereby perfects these four forms of goodness.
Just as they praise the right Dharma of these four qualities,[75]
So too is he praised by both men and gods.

简体字	正體字
2-040 能伏说清净由智悲无垢 恒共智人集王法智生长	2-040 能伏說清淨由智悲無垢 恒共智人集王法智生長
2-041 善说人难得听善言亦难 第三人最胜能疾行善教	2-041 善說人難得聽善言亦難 第三人最勝能疾行善教
2-042 若善非所爱已知应疾修 如药味虽苦乐差应强服	2-042 若善非所愛已知應疾修 如藥味雖苦樂差應強服
2-043 寿无病王位恒应思无常 次生厌怖想后专心行法	2-043 壽無病王位恒應思無常 次生厭怖想後專心行法
2-044 见决定应死死从恶见苦 智人为现乐故不应作罪	2-044 見決定應死死從惡見苦 智人為現樂故不應作罪
2-045 见一念无怖若见后时畏 若一念心安云何后不畏	2-045 見一念無怖若見後時畏 若一念心安云何後不畏
2-046 由酒遭他轻损事减身力 由痴行非事故智人断酒	2-046 由酒遭他輕損事減身力 由癡行非事故智人斷酒

8. ADDITIONAL PRACTICAL ADVICE FOR THE KING
   a. DEVELOPING WISDOM THROUGH HUMILITY, PURITY, WISDOM, AND COMPASSION

040

Insofar as he is able to be humble in discourse, to abide in purity
Made immaculate through wisdom and compassion,
And to constantly congregate with the wise,
The King's dharma and wisdom will come forth and grow.

   b. ON THE RARITY OF SWIFTLY CHANGING TO WHAT IS GOOD

041

People who discourse on what is good are rare.
Those who listen to words encouraging goodness are also rare.
A third type of person is the most superior:
It is whoever can swiftly implement teachings on goodness.

042

Even if what is good is not what one finds pleasing,
Once aware of its implications, one should swiftly cultivate it.
This is comparable to when, though a medicine is bitter,
One inclined to be cured should still force himself to take it.

   c. ON THE NEED TO CONTEMPLATE IMPERMANENCE

043

As for long life, freedom from disease, and one's position as king,
One should constantly contemplate their impermanence.
As a consequence, thoughts turn toward renunciation and alarm,
And one then focuses the mind on the practice of Dharma.

044

One perceives that he is definitely bound to die
And that death brings on sufferings arising from evil deeds.
The wise person, for the sake of happiness even in the present,
Should therefore refrain from committing any karmic offenses.[76]

045

Having already experienced moments free of fear
Followed by encounters with fearsome experiences—
Even as one now experiences moments of mental peace,
How can he fail to be apprehensive over what might follow later?[77]

   d. ON THE NEGATIVE EFFECTS OF INTOXICANTS

046

Through consuming intoxicants, one encounters others' disdain,
Brings harm to one's works, and reduces one's physical strength.
Due to the stupidity it induces, one courses in wrong endeavors.
Therefore the wise man does away with consumption of intoxicants.

简体字	正體字
2-047 围棋等嬉戏生贪瞋忧谄 诳妄恶口因故应恒远离	2-047 圍碁等嬉戲生貪瞋憂諂 誑妄惡口因故應恒遠離
2-048 婬逸过失生由想女身净 寻思女身中实无一毫净	2-048 婬逸過失生由想女身淨 尋思女身中實無一毫淨
2-049 女口涎唾器齿舌垢臭秽 鼻[11]臭由洟流目泪种类处	2-049 女口涎唾器齒舌垢臭穢 鼻[11]臭由洟流目淚種類處
2-050 腹屎尿肠器馀身骨肉聚 痴人迷可厌故贪着此[12]身	2-050 腹屎尿腸器餘身骨肉聚 癡人迷可厭故貪著此[12]身
2-051 根门最臭秽是厌恶身因 于中若生爱何缘得离欲	2-051 根門最臭穢是厭惡身因 於中若生愛何緣得離欲
2-052 譬如屎尿器猪好在中戏 于身不净门多欲戏亦尔	2-052 譬如屎尿器猪好在中戲 於身不淨門多欲戲亦爾
2-053 此门所以生为弃身土秽 痴人邪爱着不顾己善利	2-053 此門所以生為棄身土穢 癡人邪愛著不顧己善利

e. ON THE NEGATIVE EFFECTS OF GAMING AND ENTERTAINMENTS

047
Competitive gaming and other such entertainments[78]
Generate covetousness, ill-will, distress, and deviousness.
They are causes for deceptiveness, falseness, and harsh speech.
Therefore one should always keep one's distance from them.

f. ON COUNTERING LUST THROUGH REALIZING IMPURITY OF THE BODY

048
The fault of indulging lustful excess arises
From the perception that a woman's body is "pure."
If one investigates and ponders the contents of the female body,
One finds, in reality, not even one tiny part of it is pure.[79]

049
A woman's mouth is a vessel containing saliva and spittle.
Scum on the teeth and tongue is odorous and filthy.
The nasal cavity smells on account of the oozing of mucous.
And where the eyes' tears flow, various sorts of matter abide.

050
The abdominal cavity is a chamber of feces, urine, and intestines,
Whereas the rest of the body is but a mass of bones and flesh.
Because deluded persons are fooled even by what is disgusting,
They become attached by lust to this body.

051
The sense-faculty orifices are the most foul-smelling and filthy,
Thus they are the cause for disgust and loathing of the body.
If one generates affection even for them,
What then could serve as the basis for the abandoning of desire?

052
It is comparable to a pit full of feces and urine
In which the swine enjoy playing about.
When, in the impure orifices of the body,
One has much desire to sport, it's just the same.

053
The basis for the existence of these orifices
Is the need to expel the body's dirt-like waste.
Deluded persons mistakenly become affectionately attached,
Failing to regard what serves their own welfare.

2-054
汝自见一分屎尿等不净
此聚说名身云何汝生爱

2-055
赤白为生种厕汁所[13]泼养
如知身不净何意苦生爱

2-056
秽聚可憎恶臭湿皮缠裹
若能处中卧则爱着女身

2-057
若可爱可憎衰老及童女
女身皆不净汝何处生欲

2-058
设粪聚好色软滑相端正
起爱则不应爱女身亦尔

2-059
内臭极不净外皮所覆藏
是死尸种性云何见不知

2-060
皮不净如衣不可暂解浣
云何秽聚皮可[1]权时[2]汰净

2-061
画瓶满粪秽外饰若汝憎
此身秽种满云何汝不厌

简体字

2-054
汝自見一分屎尿等不淨
此聚說名身云何汝生愛

2-055
赤白為生種廁汁所[13]潑養
如知身不淨何意苦生愛

2-056
穢聚可憎惡臭濕皮纏裹
若能處中臥則愛著女身

2-057
若可愛可憎衰老及童女
女身皆不淨汝何處生欲

2-058
設糞聚好色軟滑相端正
起愛則不應愛女身亦爾

2-059
內臭極不淨外皮所覆藏
是死屍種性云何見不知

2-060
皮不淨如衣不可暫解浣
云何穢聚皮可[1]權時[2]汰淨

2-061
畫瓶滿糞穢外飾若汝憎
此身穢種滿云何汝不厭

正體字

054
You have seen for yourself a portion
Of the impurities of excrement, urine, and such.
Given it is this sort of aggregation defining the nature of the body,
How then could it be that you generate affection for it?

055
The red and white effluents attend the seeds of the body's growth[80]
Which is then nourished in the midst of fecal fluids.
If one is aware of the impurity of the body,
Why does one suffer the arising of desire for it?

056
Supposing there were a mass of filth, detestable and disgusting,
Stinking and wet, yet wrapped up in a skin.
If one could bear to lie down in the midst of that,
Then one might [sensibly] be lustfully attached to a woman's body.

057
No matter whether it be attractive, detestable,
Deteriorated with age, or that of a virgin maiden—
In every case, the female body is impure.
For which part of it then could you develop any desire?

058
Supposing there were a heap of dung, arranged in agreeable form,
Soft and slippery, presenting an appearance that seems attractive.
Were one to develop a love for it, this would not be so very fitting.
Any affection for the female body is precisely the same as this.

059
Its insides are such as would stink. They are extremely impure.
But on the outside, they are covered up, hidden by the skin.
This is of the same nature of the corpse of one deceased.
How then could one observe this and yet fail to remain aware?

060
The skin's impurity is like that of soiled robe,
But is such as one can't briefly remove and wash.
How could a skin that's used to wrap up a mass of filth
Be amenable even temporarily to being rinsed clean?

061
In the case of a painted vase full of fecal filth—
If you would detest it even though outwardly decorated—
Then what about this body, filled with various sorts of filth?
How can you not find it [equally] disgusting?

简体字	正體字
2-062 若汝憎不净云何不恶身 香华鬘饮食本净而能污	2-062 若汝憎不淨云何不惡身 香華鬘飲食本淨而能污
2-063 如汝并憎恶于自他粪秽 云何汝不厌自他不净身	2-063 如汝併憎惡於自他糞穢 云何汝不厭自他不淨身
2-064 如女身不净自身秽亦尔 是故离欲人于内外相称	2-064 如女身不淨自身穢亦爾 是故離欲人於內外相稱
2-065 九门流不净自证自浣濯 若不知不净而造爱欲论	2-065 九門流不淨自證自浣濯 若不知不淨而造愛欲論
2-066 希有极无知无惭及轻他 于最不净身何方利益汝	2-066 希有極無知無慚及輕他 於最不淨身何方利益汝
2-067 多众生因此无明覆其心 为尘欲结怨如狗鬪争粪	2-067 多眾生因此無明覆其心 為塵欲結怨如狗鬪爭糞
2-068 如搔痒谓乐不痒最安乐 如此有欲乐无欲人最乐	2-068 如搔癢謂樂不癢最安樂 如此有欲樂無欲人最樂

062
If you detest what is impure,
How can you not loathe the body?
Even perfumes and flower garlands, drinks and foods,
Though originally pure, can nonetheless be defiled by it.

063
In the same way that you are equally disgusted
By the fecal filth of both yourself and others—
Why are you not repelled
By the impure bodies of both yourself and others?

064
Just as the female body is impure,
The filth of one's own body is just the same.
Therefore, the person abandoning desire,
Gives equal weight to the inward and the outward.[81]

065
That the nine orifices ooze impurities
Is something one has witnessed oneself and cleansed for oneself.
Only if one were unaware of this impurity
Might he still justifiably compose writings extolling desire.

066
To do so involves a rare state of extreme unconsciousness,
Absence of shame, and condescension to others' intelligence.
[If you thus esteem] a body so extremely impure,
What means [of teaching] could possibly benefit you?

  g. ON THE NEGATIVE EFFECTS, ASPECTS, AND FUTILITY OF LUST
067
Many are the beings who, on account of this,
Have their minds covered over by ignorance.
Due to sensual desire, they may even become rivals,
Acting like dogs fighting over feces.

068
Just as scratching an itch might be thought pleasurable,
When having no itch is most pleasant of all,
So too it is with pleasures linked to desire,
For those free of desire are the happiest of all.

2-069
若汝思此义离欲不得成
由思欲轻故不遭婬逸过

2-070
从猎感短寿怖苦重逼恼
未来决受此故应坚行悲

2-071
何人若他见生彼极惊怖
譬粪秽污身流出毒恶蛇

2-072
是人若至彼众生得安乐
譬夏月大云田夫见欲雨

2-073
故汝舍恶法决心修善行
为自他俱得无上菩提果

2-074
是菩提根本心坚如山王
因十方际悲及无二依智

2-075
大王汝谛听此因我今说
感三十二相能庄严汝身

简体字

2-069
若汝思此義離欲不得成
由思欲輕故不遭婬逸過

2-070
從獵感短壽怖苦重逼惱
未來決受此故應堅行悲

2-071
何人若他見生彼極驚怖
譬糞穢污身流出毒惡蛇

2-072
是人若至彼眾生得安樂
譬夏月大雲田夫見欲雨

2-073
故汝捨惡法決心修善行
為自他俱得無上菩提果

2-074
是菩提根本心堅如山王
因十方際悲及無二依智

2-075
大王汝諦聽此因我今說
感三十二相能莊嚴汝身

正體字

069
If you reflect upon the meaning of this,
But do not succeed in abandoning desire,
Because ruminations focused on desire will become but slight,
You will avoid stumbling into transgressions through unbridled lust.

> h. ON THE DISASTROUS KARMIC EFFECTS OF HUNTING

070
It is from hunting that one brings on a shortness of lifespan,
The suffering of being terrorized, and repeated torments.
In the future one will definitely undergo these experiences.
Therefore one should resolutely practice compassion.

071
What sort of person is it that, when seen by others,
Produces in them extreme alarm or terror,
Like that caused by one whose body is smeared with fecal filth,
Or like that elicited by a poisonous serpent streaming venom?[82]

072
A person of this sort, when he leaves to go off somewhere else,
Produces such gladness in beings
It's comparable to when the huge summer [monsoon] clouds come
And, seeing them, the farmers all look forward to the rains.[83]

> i. ON THE NEED TO RELINQUISH EVIL AND CULTIVATE GOOD FOR THE SAKE OF BODHI

073
You should therefore relinquish the dharmas of evil
And, with decisive mind, cultivate good actions,
This for the sake of bringing to both self and others realization
Of the unsurpassed fruits of bodhi.

> j. ON THE BASES FOR THE REALIZATION OF BODHI IN COMPASSION AND WISDOM

074
The foundation of this bodhi
Is resolve as solid as the king of mountains.
It is caused by compassion as expansive as the ten directions,
And wisdom free of any bases in duality.

> k. ON THE CAUSES FOR GAINING THE THIRTY-TWO MARKS

075
Great King, may you truly listen
As I now explain these causes
Evoking the appearance of the thirty-two major marks
Which may come to adorn your body.[84]

简体字	正體字
2-076 支提圣尊人供养恒亲侍 手足宝相轮当成转轮王	**2-076** 支提聖尊人供養恒親侍 手足寶相輪當成轉輪王
2-077 手足滑柔软身大七处高 由施美饮食于他等豐足	**2-077** 手足滑柔軟身大七處高 由施美飲食於他等豐足
2-078 身圆满端直指足跟圆长 汝当感长寿由悲济死囚	**2-078** 身圓滿端直指足跟圓長 汝當感長壽由悲濟死囚
2-079 大王坚持法令清净久住 由此足安平当得成菩萨	**2-079** 大王堅持法令清淨久住 由此足安平當得成菩薩
2-080 行布施爱语利行及同利 由此指网密手足八十文	**2-080** 行布施愛語利行及同利 由此指網密手足八十文
2-081 脚趺高可爱旋毛端向上 由长不弃背本所受持法	**2-081** 脚趺高可愛旋毛端向上 由長不棄背本所受持法
2-082 由恭敬施受明处及工巧 故得鹿王[3]膊及聪明大智	**2-082** 由恭敬施受明處及工巧 故得鹿王[3]膊及聰明大智
2-083 他求自有物我疾能惠施 由此臂佣大得为世化主	**2-083** 他求自有物我疾能惠施 由此臂傭大得為世化主

076
When to the *caityas* (shrines), *āryas*, and venerable persons,
One makes offerings and constantly serves them personally,
[One plants causes for] the precious wheel mark on hands and feet
And becomes destined to rule as a wheel-turning monarch.

077
[Acquisition of] smoothness and softness of hands and feet,
And of a body that's tall and prominent in seven places
Occurs through giving exquisite food and drink
To others which, in its bounteousness, is equal to one's own.

078
A body well-rounded, full, handsomely formed, and erect—
As for digits and feet: heels are round, [fingers and toes] are long.
You will be bound to evoke the result of long life
Through compassionate rescue of prisoners bound for execution.

079
Great King, solidly supporting the Dharma,
Thus causing it to remain pure and abide for a long time—
The result of this is that one's feet will be stable and level,
While one is also bound to become a bodhisattva.

080
One practices giving, pleasing discourse,
Beneficial actions, and salutary joint endeavors.[85]
Because of this, the fingers, [at their base], are joined close by webs
While hands and feet are graced with eighty [wheel-spoke] lines.

081
The insteps are elevated and pleasing to behold,
And the tips of the bodily hairs are turned, facing upwards.
These stem from long avoiding rejecting or contravening
The Dharma which one originally accepted and upheld.

082
On account of revering, making gifts to, and taking in
People resourceful in intelligence and craftsmanship,
One thereby gains shanks like the antelope
As well as bright intelligence and great wisdom.

083
When someone else seeks something possessed by oneself
And one is then able to bestow it swiftly and with kindness—
On account of this, one gains arms which are straight and large,
And one becomes a ruler who transforms the world.

2-084
亲爱若别离菩萨令和集
此感阴藏相恒服惭羞衣

2-085
常施楼殿具细软可爱色
故感天色身润滑光微妙

2-086
由施无上护如理顺尊长
感一孔一毛白毫端严面

2-087
常说善爱语又能顺正教
上身如师子颈圆喻甘浮

2-088
看病给医药或令他[4]养护
故得腋下满千脉别百味

2-089
于自他法事常能为端首
顶骨欝尼沙横[5]竖颊匿瞿

2-090
由长时巧说实美滑善言
得八相梵音及舌根脩广

2-091
已知事实利数数为他说
得好如师子面门方可爱

084
When those formerly close and affectionate become estranged,
The bodhisattva causes them to be able to come together.
This brings as a karmic result the mark of genital concealment
And the constant possession of robes reflecting modesty and decency.

085
From always giving furnishings for buildings and halls
Which are fine, soft, and pleasing in color,
One brings as a karmic result a body of celestial appearance,
Smooth and soft, emanating a subtle and sublime radiance.

086
On account of providing unsurpassed protection
And according in a principled manner with venerables and seniors,
One evokes as a result a single hair in each hair pore
And the [mid-brow] white-hair tuft adorning one's countenance.

087
On account of always speaking good and pleasing words
While being able as well to accord with correct teachings,
One's upper body becomes like that of the lion,
The shoulders are rounded, and [the body] resembles a *nyagrodha*.[86]

088
From caring for the sick and providing physicians and medicine,
Or from ordering others to provide them care and protection,
One thereby gains the fullness in the area below the axilla
And the thousand taste channels distinguishing the hundred flavors.

089
Through service in Dharma endeavors benefiting self and other,
And through always being able to act as an upright leader,
One comes to possess the *uṣṇīṣa* crowning the skull
And has jaws which, in breadth and height, are like the lion.[87]

090
On account of being able to speak skillfully for an extended time
Words which are true, lovely, gentle, and imbued with goodness,
One gains the brahmin voice possessed of eight characteristics
Along with a tongue which is long and broad.

091
Having realized what is of genuine benefit in one's endeavors
And then repeatedly explaining this for the sake of others,
One gains the fine marks like those of the lion
And one's countenance appears square-set and pleasing to behold.

2-092
由尊他不轻随顺行正理
齿白齐必胜譬若真珠行

2-093
由数习此言谓实不两舌
故具四十齿平滑坚[6]逈净

2-094
由瞻视众生滑无贪瞋痴
眼珠青滑了睑睫如牛王

2-095
由如此略说大人相及因
转轮王菩萨美饰汝应知

2-096
随相有八十从慈悲流生
大王我不说为避多文辞

2-097
虽诸转轮王同有此相好
净明及可爱终不逮如来

2-098
从菩萨善心一念中一分
轮王相好因尚不能等此

简体字

2-092
由尊他不輕隨順行正理
齒白齊必勝譬若真珠行

2-093
由數習此言謂實不兩舌
故具四十齒平滑堅[6]逈淨

2-094
由瞻視眾生滑無貪瞋癡
眼珠青滑了瞼睫如牛王

2-095
由如此略說大人相及因
轉輪王菩薩美飾汝應知

2-096
隨相有八十從慈悲流生
大王我不說為避多文辭

2-097
雖諸轉輪王同有此相好
淨明及可愛終不逮如來

2-098
從菩薩善心一念中一分
輪王相好因尚不能等此

正體字

092
On account of honoring others and not slighting them,
Being concordant, and implementing correct principles in actions,
One's teeth are white, even, and of definite superiority,
Resembling in their appearance a strand of real pearls.

093
On account of repeated fulfillment of the import of these words
Which speak the truth and avoid divisive speech,
One thereby comes to have forty teeth
Which are even, smooth, solid, closely set, and immaculate.

094
On account of looking upon beings
With a gentleness[88] free of covetousness, hatefulness, or delusion,
One's eyes are blue and glisteningly smooth,
And one's eyelashes resemble those of the king of the bulls.

095
In a manner such as this, one explains in brief
The marks of the great man as well as their causes.
The wheel-turning king's and the Bodhisattva's[89]
Exquisite adornments are matters of which you should be aware.

l. On the Eighty Subsidiary Physical Signs
096
The subsidiary physical signs are eighty in number.
Their development flows forth from kindness and compassion.
Great King, I refrain from explaining them here
To avoid an overly lengthy composition.

m. On the Similar Marks But Deficient Causes of Wheel-Turning Sage Kings
097
Although the wheel-turning kings
Are the same in also possessing these marks and physical signs,
Still, their purity, radiance and pleasing appearance
Can never compare with those of the Tathāgata.

098
If from a bodhisattva's mind of goodness
There were to come a single measure [of cause] for each instant,
The causes for a wheel-turning king's marks and physical signs
Could not equal even one of these.

2-099

一人万亿劫修善根生长
于佛一毛相此因亦不感

2-100

诸佛与轮王相中一分等
譬如萤与日于光微有似

简体字

2-099

一人萬億劫修善根生長
於佛一毛相此因亦不感

2-100

諸佛與輪王相中一分等
譬如螢與日於光微有似

正體字

099

When a single person courses through a myriad *koṭis* of kalpas,
Cultivating the generation and growth of roots of goodness,
Considering [the requisites for] just one hair of a buddha's body,
This [person's] causal practices still could not bring that about.

100

Comparing [practices] of wheel-turning kings to those of buddhas
In relation to but a single measure of causes behind one physical sign
Would be like comparing a firefly's glow to the light of the sun.
In terms of its relative brilliance, it would barely even equal this.

宝行王正论	寶行王正論
菩提资粮品第三	菩提資糧品第三

简体字

[*]宝行王正论

菩提资粮品第三

3-001
诸佛大相好从难思福生
我今为汝说依大乘7阿舍/含

3-002
一切缘觉福有学无学福
及十方世福福如世难量

3-003
此福更十倍感佛一毛相
九万九千毛一一福皆尔

3-004
如此众多福生佛一切毛
复更百倍增方感佛一好

3-005
如是如是多一一好得成
乃至满八十随饰一大相

3-006
如是福德聚能感八十好
合更百倍增感佛一大相

正體字

[*]寶行王正論

菩提資糧品第三

3-001
諸佛大相好從難思福生
我今為汝說依大乘7阿舍/含

3-002
一切緣覺福有學無學福
及十方世福福如世難量

3-003
此福更十倍感佛一毛相
九萬九千毛一一福皆爾

3-004
如此眾多福生佛一切毛
復更百倍增方感佛一好

3-005
如是如是多一一好得成
乃至滿八十隨飾一大相

3-006
如是福德聚能感八十好
合更百倍增感佛一大相

Chapter Three

The Provisions for Gaining Enlightenment

III. Chapter 3: The Provisions for Gaining Enlightenment
   A. The Immense Merit Required for Enlightenment

001

The major marks and subsidiary physical signs of the Buddhas
Are generated from inconceivably vast merit.
I shall now describe it for you,
Doing so based upon the *āgama* scriptures of the Great Vehicle.[90]

002

The merit generated by all of the pratyekabuddhas,
The merit produced by those in training and beyond training,[91]
And the merit generated by beings in the ten directions' worlds—
That sum of merit, as with the worlds themselves, is incalculable.

003

Such merit, when multiplied by ten,
Is adequate to bring forth one body hair of a buddha.
In the case of the remaining ninety-nine thousand hairs,
The merit required for each and every one is precisely the same.

004

Such a manifold amount of merit as this
Is involved in generating all of the hairs on a buddha's body.
This [entire sum] must be increased by yet a hundred times more
To bring forth but one of a buddha's subsidiary physical signs.

005

In this fashion, through so very much [merit] as this,
Each and every one of the subsidiary physical signs is perfected.
And so this continues on till the requisites are fulfilled for all eighty
Serving as subsidiary gracing adornments for each major mark.

006

Such an accumulation of merit as this
Is able to bring forth the eighty subsidiary physical signs.
Taken all together and multiplied by one hundred,
[Such merit] brings forth one of a buddha's major marks.

简体字	正體字
3-007 如是多福德能感三十相 复更百倍增感毫如满月	3-007 如是多福德能感三十相 復更百倍增感毫如滿月
3-008 能感白毫福复更千倍增 此福感难见顶上欝尼沙	3-008 能感白毫福復更千倍增 此福感難見頂上欝尼沙
3-009 如此无量福方便说有量 于一切十方如说十倍世	3-009 如此無量福方便說有量 於一切十方如說十倍世
3-010 诸佛色身因尚如世无量 况佛法身因而当有边际	3-010 諸佛色身因尚如世無量 況佛法身因而當有邊際
3-011 世间因虽小若果大难量 佛因既无量果量云何思	3-011 世間因雖小若果大難量 佛因既無量果量云何思
3-012 诸佛有色身皆从福行起 大王佛法身由智慧行成	3-012 諸佛有色身皆從福行起 大王佛法身由智慧行成
3-013 故佛福慧行是菩提正因 故愿汝恒行菩提福慧行	3-013 故佛福慧行是菩提正因 故願汝恒行菩提福慧行

007
An amount of merit such as this
Is able to bring about [each one of] the thirty major marks.
When multiplied again by one hundred,
It brings forth the hair-tuft [at mid brow] resembling a full moon.

008
That merit able to bring about that white hair-tuft,
When multiplied again by a thousand fold—
Such a sum of merit is able to bring forth the vision-surpassing
Uṣṇīṣa [mark] atop a buddha's crown.

009
Such an incalculable amount of merit as this,
Is expediently described herein as calculable.
However, if one drew from throughout the ten directions
An amount of merit present in ten times all those worlds,

010
The causal basis for obtaining a buddha's form body
Would itself be just as incalculable as such a number of worlds.
How much the less would the causes of a buddha's Dharma body
Be such as might have any bounds?

011
If causes operative in the world, even though minor,
Are capable of generating effects so great they are incalculable,
Since the causes for buddhahood are incalculably [potent,]
How could one even conceive of the scale of their result?

B. THE FORM BODY ARISES FROM MERIT, THE DHARMA BODY FROM WISDOM

012
The possession of the form body by the Buddhas,
In every case arises from the merit-generating practices.
Great King, the Dharma body of the Buddhas
Is perfected through the wisdom-generating practices.

C. HENCE THE CORRECT CAUSES OF BUDDHAHOOD ARE MERIT AND WISDOM

013
Therefore practices generating the merit and wisdom of a buddha
Are the correct causes for the realization of bodhi.
Hence one prays that you will constantly cultivate
The practices generating the merit and wisdom leading to bodhi.

3-014
于成菩提福汝莫堕沈忧
有理及阿舍/含能令心安信

3-015
如十方无边空及地水火
有苦诸众生彼无边亦尔

3-016
此无边众生菩萨依大悲
从苦而拔济愿彼般涅盘

3-017
从发此坚心行住及卧觉
或时小放逸无量福恒流

3-018
福量如众生恒流无间隙
因果既相称故菩提不难

3-019
时节及众生菩提与福德
由此四无量菩萨坚心行

3-020
菩提虽无量因前四无量
修福慧二行云何难可得

简体字

3-014
於成菩提福汝莫墮沈憂
有理及阿舍/含能令心安信

3-015
如十方無邊空及地水火
有苦諸眾生彼無邊亦爾

3-016
此無邊眾生菩薩依大悲
從苦而拔濟願彼般涅槃

3-017
從發此堅心行住及臥覺
或時小放逸無量福恒流

3-018
福量如眾生恒流無間隙
因果既相稱故菩提不難

3-019
時節及眾生菩提與福德
由此四無量菩薩堅心行

3-020
菩提雖無量因前四無量
修福慧二行云何難可得

正體字

Chapter 3: *The Provisions for Gaining Enlightenment*

1. ONE SHOULD NOT BE DISCOURAGED BY THE AMOUNT OF MERIT REQUIRED

014
Regarding the amount of merit needed for realization of bodhi,
You must not fall into a state of discouragement.
Based on the principles involved as well as the *āgama* scriptures,[92]
One is able to cause one's mind to be established in faith.

a. BEINGS BESET BY SUFFERING ARE BOUNDLESSLY MANY

015
Just as, throughout the ten directions, there is
Boundless space and so forth, including earth, water, and fire,
So too it is with those beings beset by suffering,
For their boundlessness is just the same.[93]

b. THE BODHISATTVA VOWS TO LIBERATE THE COUNTLESS BEINGS

016
As for this boundless number of beings,
The bodhisattva, relying on the great compassion,
Extricates them, rescuing them from their suffering,
Vowing that they shall be caused to gain *parinirvāṇa*.

c. IMMEASURABLE MERIT FLOWS FROM THIS VOW

017
As a result of generating this firm resolve,
Whenever walking or standing, whenever lying down or awake,
Or even when sometimes being somewhat negligent—
Still, an incalculable amount of merit constantly flows to him.

018
Extent of merit matches the number of beings [he vows to rescue]
And it constantly flows to him without the slightest interruption.
Since the cause and the effect develop commensurately,
Realization of bodhi is not difficult to achieve.

019
The period of time, as well as the number of beings—
Bodhi itself, and also the amount of merit—
Because these four are all immeasurable,
The bodhisattva carries on his practice equipped with solid resolve.

020
Although bodhi is itself immeasurable,
The causes in the above four factors being also immeasurable,
As one courses in the two practices of cultivating merit and wisdom,
How could it be difficult to succeed in acquiring them?

简体字	正體字
3-021 福慧二种行如此无边际 菩萨身心苦故疾得消除 3-022 恶道饥渴等身苦恶业生 菩萨永离恶行善苦不生 3-023 欲瞋怖畏等心苦从痴生 由依无二智菩萨离心苦 3-024 有苦时若促难忍何况多 无苦时长远有乐云何难 3-025 身苦永不有假说有心苦 悲世间二苦故恒住生死 3-026 故菩提长时智人心不沈 为灭恶生善是时无间修 3-027 贪瞋及无明愿汝识舍离 无贪等众[1]善知应恭敬修	3-021 福慧二種行如此無邊際 菩薩身心苦故疾得消除 3-022 惡道飢渴等身苦惡業生 菩薩永離惡行善苦不生 3-023 欲瞋怖畏等心苦從癡生 由依無二智菩薩離心苦 3-024 有苦時若促難忍何況多 無苦時長遠有樂云何難 3-025 身苦永不有假說有心苦 悲世間二苦故恒住生死 3-026 故菩提長時智人心不沈 為滅惡生善是時無間修 3-027 貪瞋及無明願汝識捨離 無貪等眾[1]善知應恭敬修

Chapter 3: *The Provisions for Gaining Enlightenment*

d. Bodhisattva Sufferings Are Melted Away by Causal-Ground Practices

021
The two types of practice in garnering merit and wisdom—
Due to their being so boundless as this—
The bodhisattva's physical and mental sufferings
Are therefore swiftly melted away.

022
As for the wretched destinies, hunger, thirst, and so forth,
Such physical sufferings are produced from evil karmic actions.
Since the bodhisattva forever abandons evil
And cultivates goodness, such suffering ceases to arise in him.

023
Desire, hatefulness, fear, and so forth—
Such mental sufferings arise from delusion.
Because he relies on non-dual wisdom,
The bodhisattva leaves behind the mental sufferings.

024
When one experiences suffering, if it is pressing,
It becomes difficult to bear. How much the more so if it is excessive.
When freedom from suffering goes on for a long time,
One abides in happiness. How could that be difficult?

025
Whilst physical suffering becomes eternally non-existent for them,
The existence of mental suffering is but a conventional expression.
It is due to their compassion for the world's two types of suffering
That they constantly abide within the sphere of birth and death.

e. The Wise Are Not Discouraged by the Length of the Endeavor

026
Therefore, during that long time leading up to bodhi,
The mind of the wise person does not sink into discouragement.
So as to bring about cessation of evil and generation of goodness,
He cultivates this endeavor unremittingly during this entire time.

f. The Three Poisons and the Effects of Indulging or Abandoning Them

027
Covetousness, hatefulness, and ignorance—
One prays that you will recognize and abandon them.
Non-covetousness and the other manifold forms of goodness—
Once aware of them, one should cultivate them with reverence.

简体字	正體字
3-028 由贪生鬼道由瞋堕地狱 由痴入畜生翻此感人天	3-028 由貪生鬼道由瞋墮地獄 由癡入畜生翻此感人天
3-029 舍恶及修善此法是乐因 若是解脱法由智舍二执	3-029 捨惡及修善此法是樂因 若是解脱法由智捨二執
3-030 佛像及支提殿堂并寺庙 最胜多供具汝应敬成立	3-030 佛像及支提殿堂并寺廟 最勝多供具汝應敬成立
3-031 坐[2]宝莲花上好色微妙[3]画 一切金宝种汝应造佛像	3-031 坐[2]寶蓮花上好色微妙[3]畫 一切金寶種汝應造佛像
3-032 正法及圣众以命[4]色事护 金宝网缯盖奉献覆支提	3-032 正法及聖眾以命[4]色事護 金寶網繒蓋奉獻覆支提
3-033 金银众宝花珊瑚琉璃珠 帝释青大青金刚贡支提	3-033 金銀眾寶花珊瑚琉璃珠 帝釋青大青金剛貢支提
3-034 能说正法人以四事供养 六和敬等法常应勤修行	3-034 能說正法人以四事供養 六和敬等法常應勤修行

028
Through covetousness, one is reborn in the path of the ghosts.
Through hatefulness, one falls into the hells.
Through delusion, one enters the animal realm.
The opposite of these brings rebirth among men and gods.

029
Relinquishing evil and cultivating goodness—
These dharmas serve as the causes of happiness.
As for what serves as the dharma conducing to liberation,
It is relinquishing through wisdom the two types of attachment.[94]

    g. CAUSAL-GROUND BODHISATTVA PRACTICES AND THEIR POSITIVE EFFECTS
        1) FACILITATION OF THE ESTABLISHMENT OF DHARMA

030
Images of the Buddha as well as *caityas* (shrines)—
Halls together with monasteries and temples—
And also numerous superior-quality items presented as offerings—
You should respectfully see to the establishment of such things.

031
Portraying him sitting atop a precious lotus blossom,
In subtle and marvelous paintings done in fine colors,
And in likenesses created using all types of gold and gems—
You should see to the creation of such images of the Buddha.

032
Regarding right Dharma as well as the community of the Āryas,
They should, by edict, be materially served and protected.
Creating pavilions constructed with latticing of gold and jewels,
One should present these as offerings to cover the *caityas* (shrines).

033
With gold, silver, and the many kinds of blossoms made of jewels—
With carnelian, crystal, and pearls—
With *indranīla* sapphires, with *mahānīla* sapphires,
And with diamonds—make such offerings in tribute to the *caityas*.

034
To those able to proclaim right Dharma,
Make offerings of the four requisites.
The six bases of harmonious respectfulness and other such dharmas
Should be constantly and diligently cultivated.

3-035
于尊恭敬听勤事而侍护
菩萨必应行亡后亦供养

3-036
于天外道众不应亲事礼
因无知邪信莫事恶知识

3-037
佛阿含及论书写读诵施
亦惠纸笔墨汝应修此福

3-038
于国起学堂雇师供学士
兴建永基业汝行为长慧

3-039
解医巧历数皆为立田畴
润老小病苦于国有济益

3-040
起诸道伽蓝园塘湖亭屋
于中给生具草蓐饮食薪

3-041
于小大国土应起寺亭馆
远路乏水浆造井池施饮

简体字

3-035
於尊恭敬聽勤事而侍護
菩薩必應行亡後亦供養

3-036
於天外道眾不應親事禮
因無知邪信莫事惡知識

3-037
佛阿含及論書寫讀誦施
亦惠紙筆墨汝應修此福

3-038
於國起學堂雇師供學士
興建永基業汝行為長慧

3-039
解醫巧曆數皆為立田疇
潤老小病苦於國有濟益

3-040
起諸道伽藍園塘湖亭屋
於中給生具草蓐飲食薪

3-041
於小大國土應起寺亭館
遠路乏水漿造井池施飲

正體字

035
To those who are venerable, one should listen with reverence,
Diligently serving, attending to, and protecting them.
The bodhisattva must certainly carry out
The memorial ceremonies, making offerings then as well.

036
As regards theistic and other non-Buddhist communities,
One should not personally serve them or ceremonially revere them.
Because the unaware might erroneously place faith in them,
One must not render any service to bad spiritual guides.

037
The *āgamas* of the Buddha as well as the treatises
Should be copied, studied, recited, and given to others.
Also, one should bestow with kindness the paper, pens, and ink.
You should cultivate these sorts of meritorious endeavors.

    2) FACILITATION OF EDUCATION

038
Erect halls of learning throughout the country,
Hire teachers, contribute grants to scholars,
And promote the establishment of perpetual endowments.
By implementing these things, you will increase your wisdom.

    3) PROMOTE MEDICINE, SCIENCE, AGRICULTURE, WELFARE, EMERGENCY SERVICES

039
Promote understanding of medical skills and the calendar,
In all cases work for the establishment of agriculture,
Ease the suffering of the elderly, children, and the sick,
And ensure that rescue services are provided throughout the country.

    4) EASING THE HARDSHIP OF TRAVEL

040
Establish *saṅghārāmas* along the roads,[95]
As well as parks, ponds and reservoirs, rest pavilions, and lodging.
Make available therein provisions for the needs of beings,[96]
Including fodder, bedding mats, drink, food, and fuel.

    5) ESTABLISHMENT OF TEMPLES, REST PAVILIONS, INNS

041
Throughout the lands of the small and large states,
One should erect temples, rest pavilions, and inns.
On roads across great distances wherein drinking water is scarce,
Establish wells and water ponds providing a chance to drink.

3-042
病苦无依贫下姓怖畏等
依慈悲摄受勤心安立彼

3-043
随时新饮食果菜及新谷
大众及须者未施莫先用

3-044
屣繐瓶钩镊针[5]綖及扇等
[6]荃提寝息具应施寺亭馆

3-045
三果及三辛蜜糖[7]酥眼药
恒应安息省书呪及药方

3-046
涂首身药油澡[8]盘灯魦果
水器及刀斧应给亭馆中

3-047
米谷麻饮食糖膏等相应
恒置阴凉处及净水满器

3-048
于蚁鼠穴门饮食谷糖等
愿令可信人日日分布散

简体字

3-042
病苦無依貧下姓怖畏等
依慈悲攝受勤心安立彼

3-043
隨時新飲食果菜及新穀
大眾及須者未施莫先用

3-044
屣繐瓶鉤鑷針[5]綖及扇等
[6]荃提寢息具應施寺亭館

3-045
三果及三辛蜜糖[7]酥眼藥
恒應安息省書呪及藥方

3-046
塗首身藥油澡[8]盤燈魦果
水器及刀斧應給亭館中

3-047
米穀麻飲食糖膏等相應
恒置陰涼處及淨水滿器

3-048
於蟻鼠穴門飲食穀糖等
願令可信人日日分布散

正體字

6) Aid to the Sick, the Poor, the Lower Classes

042
For those suffering with illness, the poor with no one to rely on,
The lower classes, those who live in fear, and other such persons—
By resort to kindness and compassion, draw them in, accept them,
And, with diligent concern, establish them in stable circumstances.

7) Food Offerings to the Religious Community and the Needy

043
Seasonally fresh foods and beverages,
Fruits, vegetables, and recently-harvested grains—
[Bestow them on] the Great Community and those in need,
Not consuming any yourself until you've first provided for them.[97]

8) Stocking of Temples, Rest Pavilions, and Inns with Appropriate Supplies

044
Sandals, umbrellas, jugs, water-drawing hooks, tweezers,
Needles and thread, fans, and other such items, including
Mosquito netting and accouterments for taking the night's rest—
One should provide these for temples, rest pavilions, and inns.

045
The three types of fruit, the three types of pungent herbs,
Honey, sugar, curds, and eye medicines
Should always be supplied for comfort and relief during calamities,
While one also distributes copies of mantras and medical formulae.

046
Medicinal oils for application on the head and body,
Bathing tubs, lanterns, cereals and fruits,
Water vessels, knives and axes—
These should be provided in rest pavilions and inns.

047
Rice, the grains, sesame, drink, food,
Sugar syrups, and other such provisions—
One should see that they are always placed in shaded, cool locations
Together with containers full of pure water.

9) Compassionate Treatment Even of Animals, Insects, Ghosts, etc.

048
At the openings of the burrows of insects and rodents,
Place food and drink, grains, sugar, and other such provisions.
May trustworthy people be ordered to take on these tasks
So that, each and every day, these things are widely distributed.

简体字	正體字
3-049 如意前后食恒施于饿鬼 狗鼠鸟蚁等愿汝恒施食	3-049 如意前後食恒施於餓鬼 狗鼠鳥蟻等願汝恒施食
3-050 灾疫饥饿时水旱及贼难 国败须济度愿汝恒拯恤	3-050 災疫飢餓時水旱及賊難 國敗須濟度願汝恒拯恤
3-051 田夫绝农业愿给粮种具 随时蠲租税轻微受调敛	3-051 田夫絕農業願給糧種具 隨時蠲租稅輕微受調斂
3-052 施物济贫[1]债出息不长轻 直防许休偃以时接宾客	3-052 施物濟貧[1]債出息不長輕 直防許休偃以時接賓客
3-053 境内外劫盗方便断令息 随时₂遗/遣商侣平物价钧调	3-053 境內外劫盜方便斷令息 隨時₂遺/遣商侶平物價鈞調
3-054 八座等判事自如理观察 事能利万姓恒恭敬修行	3-054 八座等判事自如理觀察 事能利萬姓恒恭敬修行
3-055 应作何自利如汝恒敬思 利他云何成如此汝急思	3-055 應作何自利如汝恒敬思 利他云何成如此汝急思

049
As you wish, either before or after eating,
Always make an offering to the hungry ghosts.
To the dogs, rodents, birds, insects, and the rest,
Pray, may you also always provide them food.

    10) THE IMPORTANCE OF EMERGENCY RESCUE SERVICES

050
At times of natural disasters, pestilence, famine,
Floods, drought, difficulties wrought by insurgents,
And when states are defeated—it is essential to rescue victims.
One prays you will always provide relief and be motivated by pity.

    11) ON THE NEED TO SUPPORT FARMERS AND AGRICULTURE

051
When farmers have had agricultural livelihood interrupted,
One prays they will be supplied with seed grain and planting tools,
While, as befits the time, one will forgive rents and taxes
And reduce the number affected by military draft and levies.

    12) POVERTY RELIEF; RESTRAINT IN MILITARY ENDEAVORS; USING EXPERT ADVICE

052
Bestow whatever things may rescue the poor and debt-ridden.
Allow relief from interest through freezing or reducing loan rates.
In military redress and defense, allow ceasefire and demobilization.
As befits the time, welcome experts offering services to the Court.

    13) QUELLING CRIME; PROMOTING TRADE; ENSURING FAIRNESS IN PRICES AND TAXES

053
As regards banditry within or beyond the borders,
Institute expedients to interrupt it and ensure its cessation.
Adapting to the times, send out[98] missions promoting trade,
Control the price of goods, and ensure household taxes are fair.

    14) OVERSIGHT OF OFFICIALS; GIVING PRECEDENCE TO UNIVERSAL BENEFIT

054
In decisions on matters of state, the eight[99] cabinet-level ministers
Should be subject to your personal and principled oversight.
In public works, those beneficial to the myriad families
Should be constantly and respectfully instituted and carried out.

    15) CARE IN MATTERS OF SELF-BENEFIT; URGENCY IN MATTERS BENEFITING OTHERS

055
As for what one should do that redounds to one's own benefit,
May this accord with your constant and reverential contemplation.
As for how one is to see to the welfare of others,
You should subject this matter to urgent contemplation.[100]

简体字	正體字
3-056 地水风火等草药及野树 如此或暂时受他无碍策	3-056 地水風火等草藥及野樹 如此或暫時受他無礙策
3-057 七步顷起心为[3]舍内外财 菩萨福德成难量如虚空	3-057 七步頃起心為[3]捨內外財 菩薩福德成難量如虛空
3-058 童女好色严惠施求得者 故获陀罗尼能持一切法	3-058 童女好色嚴惠施求得者 故獲陀羅尼能持一切法
3-059 爱色具庄严并一切生具 施八万童女释迦佛昔时	3-059 愛色具莊嚴并一切生具 施八萬童女釋迦佛昔時
3-060 光明种种色衣服庄严具 花香等应施依悲惠求者	3-060 光明種種色衣服莊嚴具 花香等應施依悲惠求者
3-061 若人离此缘于法无安行 则应施与之过此后莫惠	3-061 若人離此緣於法無安行 則應施與之過此後莫惠

16) On Caring for Natural Resources
056
As for matters concerning earth, water, wind, fire, and such,
Including the grasses, herbs, and wilderness trees—
Issues of this sort may, for a limited time,
Benefit from reviewing others' unconstrained policy proposals.

17) On Giving
057
At the moment of his seventh step, he conceived the aspiration
To relinquish all inward and outward wealth.
The Bodhisattva's perfection of meritorious qualities
Is as inconceivable in its vastness as empty space itself.[101]

a) On Royal Giving Through Facilitating Marriages
058
Virgin maidens, their beauty gracefully adorned—
One may, with kindness, bestow them on their suitors.
One thereby comes into possession of the *dhāraṇīs*
Through which one is enabled to embrace all dharmas.[102]

b) Shakyamuni Buddha's Causal-Ground Precedent
059
Those of lovely form, completely and elegantly adorned,
Together with everything appropriate to a dowry—
He facilitated bestowal of eight myriads of such virgin maidens.
This was done by Shakyamuni Buddha in the course of earlier eras.

c) On Gifts Enhancing the Ceremony
060
Providing radiant light in a spectrum of hues,
Clothing, robes, the means of graceful adornment,
Flowers, perfumes, and such—one should bestow them
Out of compassion and kindness for those who would seek them.[103]

18) On Assisting the Worthy and Dealing with the Unworthy
061
Where there are persons who, absent a particular condition,
Could not establish themselves in the practice of Dharma,
Then one should bestow that beneficence on them,
But, beyond this, one must not show them any further kindness.[104]

简体字	正體字
3-062 毒亦许施彼若此能利他 甘露不许施若此损害他	3-062 毒亦許施彼若此能利他 甘露不許施若此損害他
3-063 若蛇啮人指佛亦听则除 或佛教利他逼恼亦可行	3-063 若蛇嚙人指佛亦聽則除 或佛教利他逼惱亦可行
3-064 固谨持正法及能说法人 恭敬听受法或以法施他	3-064 固謹持正法及能說法人 恭敬聽受法或以法施他
3-065 莫爱世赞叹恒乐出俗法 如立自体德[4]于他亦如此	3-065 莫愛世讚歎恒樂出俗法 如立自體德[4]於他亦如此
3-066 [*]于闻莫知足及思修实义 于师报恩施应敬行莫恪	3-066 [*]於聞莫知足及思修實義 於師報恩施應敬行莫恪
3-067 莫读外邪论但起諍慢故 不应赞自德怨德亦可赞	3-067 莫讀外邪論但起諍慢故 不應讚自德怨德亦可讚
3-068 莫显他密事及恶心两舌 自于他有过如理观悔露	3-068 莫顯他密事及惡心兩舌 自於他有過如理觀悔露

062
[In medicine], it may be allowable to give someone a toxin
If, by doing so, one is able to provide them a beneficial outcome.
So too, it may be forbidden to provide someone ambrosia (*amṛta*)
If, by doing so, one may wreak harm on others.[105]

063
In a case where a snake had bitten a person's finger,
The Buddha himself allowed that it might be best to amputate.
The Buddha taught that in some cases, where it benefits others,
One may subject someone to pressure even to the point of vexation.[106]

> 19) On Supporting, Listening to, and Giving Right Dharma

064
One should be solid and conscientious in support of right Dharma
As well as those persons able to proclaim the Dharma.
One should reverently listen to and accept the Dharma,
While at times also using the Dharma in one's giving to others.

> 20) Prefer Transcendence to Praise; Require Fine Qualities in Friends

065
Do not crave the praises of the worldly,
Rather always find happiness in dharmas surpassing the mundane.
Just as one requires embodiment of meritorious qualities in himself,
So too should this be so in one's relations with others.

> 21) Cultivate Three Kinds of Wisdom; Generously Repay the Guru's Kindness

066
Never become self-satisfied in learning [about Dharma],
In contemplating it, and in meditating on its genuine meaning.[107]
In giving proffered in repayment of the guru's kindness,
One should do it with reverence and one must avoid miserliness.

> 22) Don't Study Non-Buddhist Treatises; Don't Indulge in Self-Praise

067
One must not study the erroneous treatises of the non-Buddhists,
For they lead only to development of disputation and arrogance.
One should not praise one's own meritorious qualities,
But nonetheless may praise meritorious qualities in adversaries.

> 23) Observe Right Speech; Repent Transgressions Against Others

068
Do not expose the secrets of others
Or engage in divisive speech provoked by evil thoughts.
Where one has transgressed against others,
Reflect on it with reason while also repenting of it and revealing it.

简体字	正體字
3-069 若由此过失智者诃责他 自须离此失有能拔济他	3-069 若由此過失智者訶責他 自須離此失有能拔濟他
3-070 他辱己莫瞋即观宿恶业 莫报对他恶为后不受苦	3-070 他辱己莫瞋即觀宿惡業 莫報對他惡為後不受苦
3-071 于他应作恩莫希彼报答 唯自应受苦共求众受乐	3-071 於他應作恩莫希彼報答 唯自應受苦共求眾受樂
3-072 若得5夫/天富贵自高不应作 遭枉如饿鬼莫起下悲行	3-072 若得5夫/天富貴自高不應作 遭枉如餓鬼莫起下悲行
3-073 假设失王位或死由实言 亦恒说此语无实利默然	3-073 假設失王位或死由實言 亦恒說此語無實利默然
3-074 如言如此行愿汝坚行善 因此好名遍自在成胜量	3-074 如言如此行願汝堅行善 因此好名遍自在成勝量

24) ON THE NECESSITY OF ABANDONING FAULTS
069
If, on account of a fault such as this,
The wise would rebuke someone,
One must abandon such faults himself,
And, wherever possible, save others [from falling into such faults].

25) ON RESTRAINT FROM HATRED AND VENGEFULNESS
070
When defamed by others, one must not become hateful.
One should instead contemplate it as past-life bad karma.
Do not act vengefully in response to another's evils.
Thus one avoids enduring suffering later on.

26) ON THE NEED FOR KINDNESS WITHOUT EXPECTATION OF REQUITAL
071
Relations with others should be motivated by kindness.
Hence one must not wish that they respond with any gratitude.
It is only in oneself that one should acquiesce in suffering,
While one strives with others that all might enjoy happiness.

27) ON THE NEED TO AVOID ARROGANCE AND INDULGENCE IN SELF-PITY
072
Even were one to gain the wealth and noble birth of the gods,[108]
One should nonetheless refrain from arrogance.
Even were one to suffer injustices like those of the hungry ghosts,[109]
One must still not indulge in self-pity.

28) ON UNCOMPROMISING DEDICATION TO TRUTHFULNESS
073
Even if one might lose the throne
Or be executed as a result of speaking the truth,
Still, one should always utter this sort of speech.
Where it produces no genuine benefit, remain silent.

29) ON CONSISTENCY, DEDICATION TO GOODNESS AND THEIR BENEFITS
074
Just as one speaks, so too must one act.
One prays you will remain solid in the practice of goodness.
On account of this, a fine reputation will spread everywhere
And, with natural ease, you will become supremely eminent.

3-075
应作熟简择后则依理行
莫由信他作须自了实义

3-076
若依理行善好名遍十方
王侯续不断王富乐转大

3-077
死缘百一种寿命因不多
此因或死缘故恒应修善

3-078
若人恒行善是所得安乐
于自他若等此善乐圆足

3-079
依法为性人卧觉常安乐
梦中见善事由内无过恶

3-080
若人养父母恭[6]奉自家尊
恭善人用财忍辱有大度

3-081
软语不两舌实言同止乐
此九天帝因尽寿应修行

简体字

3-075
應作熟簡擇後則依理行
莫由信他作須自了實義

3-076
若依理行善好名遍十方
王侯續不斷王富樂轉大

3-077
死緣百一種壽命因不多
此因或死緣故恒應修善

3-078
若人恒行善是所得安樂
於自他若等此善樂圓足

3-079
依法為性人臥覺常安樂
夢中見善事由內無過惡

3-080
若人養父母恭[6]奉自家尊
恭善人用財忍辱有大度

3-081
軟語不兩舌實言同止樂
此九天帝因盡壽應修行

正體字

Chapter 3: *The Provisions for Gaining Enlightenment*

30) On Planning, Principled Actions, and Direct Knowledge of Realities

075
In deciding what should be done, subject it to thorough analysis.
Afterwards, rely on right principle in carrying it out.
Do not act solely on the basis of trusting someone else.
It is essential to entirely comprehend the true meaning oneself.

076
If one relies on right principle in carrying out what is good,
One's fine reputation will spread throughout the ten directions.
Thus the King's reign will continue without interruption,
Whereas the King's wealth and happiness will grow ever greater.

31) On the Fragility of Life and the Need for Dedication to Goodness

077
The conditions producing death are of a hundred and one kinds
Even while the causes for long life are not very many.
Because those very causes may become the conditions of death,
One should therefore constantly cultivate goodness.

078
If a person is constant in the practice of goodness,
And if this happiness thus gained
Is shared equally between self and others,
This happiness flowing from goodness is thereby perfected.

32) On the Auspiciousness Flowing from Reliance on Dharma

079
For those who by their very nature rely on the Dharma,
Whether lying down to rest or awake, they are always happy.
They see auspicious occurrences in their dreams
Because they are personally free of any faults or evils.[110]

33) The Nine Causes for Becoming Ruler of the Gods

080
If one sees to the care of one's father and mother,
Respectfully serves those honored in one's own family,
Respects good people, makes good use of material wealth,
Possesses magnanimous patience,

081
And if one remains gentle in speech, refrains from divisive speech,
Speaks the truth, and abides happily in the company of others—
These are the nine causes for becoming the ruler of the gods.
One should cultivate their practice to the very end of one's life.

3-082
由昔行九法天主感帝位
时时处法堂至今恒说此

3-083
一日三时施美食三百器
福不及刹那行慈百分一

3-084
天人等爱护日夜受喜乐
免怨火毒[7]杖是行慈现果

3-085
无功用获财后生于色界
得慈十功德若人未解脱

3-086
教一切众生坚发菩提心
菩萨德如山菩提心牢固

3-087
由信离八难因戒生善道
数修真如空得善无放逸

3-088
无谄得念根恒思得慧根
恭敬得义理护法感宿命

简体字

3-082
由昔行九法天主感帝位
時時處法堂至今恒說此

3-083
一日三時施美食三百器
福不及刹那行慈百分一

3-084
天人等愛護日夜受喜樂
免怨火毒[7]杖是行慈現果

3-085
無功用獲財後生於色界
得慈十功德若人未解脫

3-086
教一切眾生堅發菩提心
菩薩德如山菩提心牢固

3-087
由信離八難因戒生善道
數修真如空得善無放逸

3-088
無諂得念根恒思得慧根
恭敬得義理護法感宿命

正體字

082
It is on account of past practice of these nine dharmas
That the rulers of the gods gained their imperial stations.
For ages they abide within the hall of Dharma,
And, even in the present, constantly proclaim these very practices.

34) THE MERIT-GENERATING POWER AND TEN MARVELOUS EFFECTS OF KINDNESS
083
Even if one made an offering three times a day
Of three hundred dishes of exquisite cuisine,
Such merit couldn't approach that produced in a *kṣaṇa*'s instant
Of acting with kindness. Not even a hundredth could thereby arise.

084
One enjoys the affection and protection of gods, men, and others.[111]
One experiences joy and bliss both day and night.
And one avoids affliction by adversaries, fire, poison, and beatings.
These are the present-life fruits of the practice of kindness.

085
Even without effort, one gains material wealth
And, in the future, gains rebirth in the form realm [heavens].[112]
One obtains in reward the ten qualities associated with kindness.[113]
This is what shall occur if one hasn't already gained liberation.

35) THE MERIT-GENERATING POWER OF INSPIRING RESOLVE TO GAIN ENLIGHTENMENT
086
Through instructing all beings
To generate firm resolve on the realization of bodhi,
The merit of the bodhisattva becomes as massive as a mountain
And his own resolve on bodhi becomes enduringly solid.

36) THE IMPORTANT BODHISATTVA QUALITIES & PRACTICES AND THEIR EFFECTS
a) FAITH, MORAL VIRTUE, EMPTINESS, CONSISTENT GOODNESS
087
On account of faith, one abandons the eight difficulties.[114]
By observing the moral precepts, one is born in the good destinies.
Through repeated practice in realizing true suchness and emptiness,
One achieves goodness free of negligence.

b) NON-DEVIOUSNESS, CONTEMPLATION, REVERENCE, DHARMA-PROTECTION
088
By absence of deviousness, one gains the mindfulness root-faculty.
By constant contemplation, one gains the wisdom root-faculty.
Through reverence, one gains realization of right principles.
From protecting the Dharma, one gains knowledge of past lives.

3-089
布施听闻法或不障他闻
疾得如所爱与佛相值遇

3-090
无贪作事成不悭财物长
离慢招上品法忍得总持

3-091
由行五实施及惠无怖畏
非诸骂能辱故感大胜力

3-092
支提列灯行幽暗秉火烛
布施续明油故得净天眼

3-093
供养支提时即设鼓声乐
[1]蠡角等妙音故获净天耳

3-094
于他失默然不谈人德阙
随顺护彼意故得他心智

简体字

3-089
布施聽聞法或不障他聞
疾得如所愛與佛相值遇

3-090
無貪作事成不慳財物長
離慢招上品法忍得總持

3-091
由行五實施及惠無怖畏
非諸罵能辱故感大勝力

3-092
支提列燈行幽闇秉火燭
布施續明油故得淨天眼

3-093
供養支提時即設鼓聲樂
[1]蠡角等妙音故獲淨天耳

3-094
於他失默然不談人德闕
隨順護彼意故得他心智

正體字

c) Facilitating Others' Access to Dharma
089
From giving others the opportunity to hear Dharma,
Or from not presenting any obstacles to those wishing to hear it,
One will have circumstances swiftly accord with one's wishes
And one will succeed in directly encountering the Buddhas.

37) Non-Covetousness, Non-Miserliness, Non-Arrogance, Dharmas-Patience
090
Through non-covetousness, one's endeavors are bound to succeed.
Through non-miserliness, one's material wealth grows abundant.
By abandoning arrogance, one becomes bound for superior rank.
Through dharma patience, one gains complete retention (*dhāraṇī*).[115]

38) Five Types of Genuine Giving and Associated Giving of Fearlessness
091
On account of practicing the five types of genuine giving
Together with that kindliness which bestows fearlessness,[116]
One becomes such as no form of vilification can defame,
And one thereby brings about great overwhelming power.

39) Causes Generating the Six Superknowledges
a) Causes Generating the Heavenly Eye
092
From stringing lines of lanterns at the *caityas*,
By setting up torches there to dispel deep darkness,
And through giving oil for continuous illumination,
One thereby brings about purification of the heavenly eye.

b) Causes Generating the Heavenly Ear
093
When making offerings at the *caityas*,
By just then performing music with the sounds of drums,
Conches, horns, and other sublime tones,
One thereby brings about purification of the heavenly ear.

c) Causes Generating Knowledge of Others' Thoughts
094
From remaining silent about the faults of others,
Through refraining from discussing people's defects in virtue,
And from compliantly keeping the thoughts of others secure,
One thereby develops the knowledge of others' thoughts.

简体字	正體字
3-095 由施徙舟乘运致羸乏人 恭谨瞻尊长故获如意通	3-095 由施徙舟乘運致羸乏人 恭謹瞻尊長故獲如意通
3-096 令他忆法事及正法句义 或净心施法故感宿命智	3-096 令他憶法事及正法句義 或淨心施法故感宿命智
3-097 由知真实义谓诸法无性 故得第六通最胜是₂流/漏尽	3-097 由知真實義謂諸法無性 故得第六通最勝是₂流/漏盡
3-098 平等悲相应由修如实智 故自得成佛恒解脱众生	3-098 平等悲相應由修如實智 故自得成佛恒解脫眾生
3-099 由种种净愿故佛土清净 众宝献支提故放无边光	3-099 由種種淨願故佛土清淨 眾寶獻支提故放無邊光
3-100 如此业及果已知义相应 故应修利他即菩萨自利	3-100 如此業及果已知義相應 故應修利他即菩薩自利

d) Causes Generating Psychic Power

095
On account of providing boats and carts as means of conveyance
To assist transport of weak and destitute people,
And by respectful attentiveness to those venerable and senior,
One thereby acquires the psychic power superknowledge.

e) Causes Generating Knowledge of Past Lives

096
Through leading others to bear in mind Dharma-related matters,
Including the meaning of statements in right-Dharma scriptures,
And by giving Dharma with a pure mind,
One thereby brings about the knowledge of past lives.

f) Causes Generating Cessation of Outflow Impurities

097
Through realizing the genuine reality-based meaning,
Namely that all dharmas have no inherently-existing nature,
One thereby gains the sixth of the superknowledges.
This most supreme of them is cessation of outflow impurities.[117]

40) Compassion and Wisdom as Causes of Bodhi and Liberation of Beings

098
By embodying uniformly equal compassion
Through cultivating reality-concordant wisdom,
One thereby naturally gains realization of buddhahood
And constantly carries on the liberation of beings.

41) Vows as Causes for Pure Buddhaland; Jewels as Causes of Radiance

099
On account of making the different types of pure vows,
One thereby brings about purification of one's buddhaland.
On account of offering up the many sorts of jewels to the *caityas*,
One produces the radiance of boundless light.

42) Encouragement to Cultivate the Bodhisattva's Benefit of Others

100
As for karmic actions and effects such as these,
Having understood them in a way consistent with their meaning,
One should therefore cultivate those practices benefiting others.
For the bodhisattva, they are the same as those benefiting himself.

宝行王正论

正教王品第四

4-001
王若行非法或作非道理
事王人亦赞故好恶难知

4-002
亦有世间人非爱善难教
何况大国王能受善人语

4-003
我今愍念汝及悲诸世间
故我善教汝实益若非爱

4-004
真滑有义利依时由慈悲
佛令教弟子故我为汝说

4-005
若听闻实语应住于无瞋
可取必须受如浴受净水

Chapter Four
Guidance Especially for Rulers

IV. Chapter 4: Guidance Especially for Rulers
   A. Nāgārjuna's Introduction to His Instructions
      1. Difficulties Specific to Rulers
         a. Unreliability of Underlings

001
If a king practices what is contrary to Dharma
Or perhaps acts in contradiction to principles according with the Path,
Those serving the king will nonetheless praise those deeds.
Hence it may be difficult to distinguish good from bad.

         b. Disinclination to Accept Remonstrative Teaching

002
Even common worldly people,
Not being fond of goodness, may be difficult to instruct.
How much the less might a great country's king
Be able to accept the counsel of those devoted to goodness?

         c. My Motivation in Offering Advice

003
Because I feel sympathetic concern for you
And because I feel compassion for all in this world
I therefore attempt here to skillfully instruct you
In the genuinely beneficial, even though you may not find it pleasing.

         d. The Buddha's Standard for Correctness of Instruction

004
Teachings should be true, gently presented, meaningful, salutary,
Timely, and motivated by kindness and compassion.
The Buddha enjoins us to instruct disciples in this manner.
Guided by that, I offer these teachings for you.

         e. The Ideal Stance for a Recipient of Teachings

005
When listening to discourse reflecting reality,
One should abide in a state free from anger.
It is essential to accept in practice whatever one is able to grasp.
This is just as when bathing where one accepts the use of clean water.

4-006
我今说善言现来有利益
汝知应受行为自及于世

4-007
由昔施贫苦故今感富财
因贪不知恩废施无更得

4-008
世间唯路粮不雇无人负
由施[3]供下品未来荷百倍

4-009
愿汝发大心恒兴建大事
若行大心事是人得大果

4-010
小意[4]陿狭劣[5]王心愿未曾触
好名吉祥事三宝依应作

4-011
望王[6]后等毛若事非汝法
死亦起恶名王不作最胜

简体字

4-006
我今說善言現來有利益
汝知應受行為自及於世

4-007
由昔施貧苦故今感富財
因貪不知恩廢施無更得

4-008
世間唯路糧不雇無人負
由施[3]供下品未來荷百倍

4-009
願汝發大心恒興建大事
若行大心事是人得大果

4-010
小意[4]陿狹劣[5]王心願未曾觸
好名吉祥事三寶依應作

4-011
望王[6]后等毛若事非汝法
死亦起惡名王不作最勝

正體字

Chapter 4: *Guidance Especially for Rulers*

f. Good and Beneficial Teaching Should Be Accepted for the Sake of All
006
I now set forth words devoted to goodness
Which can be beneficial both now and in the future.
On knowing their import, you should accept them in practice,
Doing so for your own sake and for the sake of the world.

B. The Instructions Proper
1. On the Importance of Giving and Accomplishing Great Endeavors
a. Giving As the Cause of Present Wealth; Greed As the Cause of Its Loss
007
Through giving done in the past to the poor and the suffering,
One has brought about the wealth one enjoys in the present.
Through covetousness, failure to act out of a sense of gratitude,
And neglecting giving, one might be caused to never obtain it again.

b. Present Giving As the Cause of Future Ease
008
In the world, considering only the provisions for travel,
If one fails to hire anyone, nobody will take up your burden.
Still, through giving provided [now] to those of lesser station,
They gratefully bear a hundred times greater burden in the future.

c. Exhortation to Great Resolve, Great Endeavors, Great Future Results
009
One prays that you will bring forth the great resolve
And constantly promote the establishment of great endeavors.
Where one engages in endeavors flowing from the great resolve,
Such a person will succeed in gaining the great result.

1) Encouragement to Undertake Fine Endeavors Guided by the Three Jewels
010
[Endeavors] such as insular and inferior kings with lesser intellects
Would not even conceive of in their aspirations—
Auspicious endeavors conducing to a fine reputation—
On should undertake them in reliance on the Three Jewels.[118]

####### a) On the Need for Right Motivation in One's Endeavors
011
If one becomes concerned with inspiring awe in other monarchs,[119]
But one's works contradict your own Dharma,
Then, even in death, one might still develop a terrible reputation
As the king who failed to accomplish what is most superior.

4-012

广大事能起大人希有用
能障下人愿以命成此事

4-013

无自[7]在弃物[8]只身入未来
若于法安财前至逆相待

4-014

先帝诸产业弃本属新王
能为前王生法乐好名不

4-015

用财受现喜若施感来乐
非此二唐失唯生苦无欢

4-016

将终欲行施臣碍失自在
祚绝故舍爱随新王乐欲

4-017

若舍一切物汝今安弘法
亦常在死缘譬如风中灯

4-012

廣大事能起大人希有用
能障下人願以命成此事

4-013

無自[7]在棄物[8]隻身入未來
若於法安財前至逆相待

4-014

先帝諸產業棄本屬新王
能為前王生法樂好名不

4-015

用財受現喜若施感來樂
非此二唐失唯生苦無歡

4-016

將終欲行施臣礙失自在
祚絕故捨愛隨新王樂欲

4-017

若捨一切物汝今安弘法
亦常在死緣譬如風中燈

b) On the Need to Select Endeavors Carefully

012

If one is able to initiate expansively great endeavors
Which serve those rare uses conceived of by great men,
And if one is able to block the aspirations of inferior persons,
One should utilize one's edict to accomplish such endeavors.

2. On the Correct and Timely Uses of Wealth
a. On How One May Ensure Future-Life Affluence

013

Bereft of any personal freedom, one casts off all possessions
And, as a solitary individual, proceeds on into the future.
If one establishes one's wealth in the Dharma,
It proceeds on ahead, welcomes one, and awaits [one's future use].

b. On Death's Severance of the Benefits of Possessions

014

As for the assets of previous emperors,
Having cast aside possessions, they belong then to the new king.
Are they able then to provide to a former king,
Dharma, happiness, or fine reputation, or not?

c. Wealth's Role in Present or Future Happiness

015

One may use wealth for joy in the present
Or, through using it in giving, for one's happiness in the future.
Where not used for either of these two, it is bound to be lost in vain,
For it will only generate suffering and an absence of bliss.

d. Why Waiting till the End to Give Won't Work

016

If one waits till the end, only then aspiring to practice giving,
The officials will interfere, and one will lose independent control.
Because the reign is to be cut short, they withdraw their affections,
And then accord instead with whatever will please the new king.

e. Given the Inevitability of Death, Be Devoted to Propagating Dharma

017

Since one is bound in any case to relinquish all possessions,
You would best now commit them to propagation of Dharma,
For one still always abides in conditions conducing to death
And so is comparable in this to a lantern flame set out in the wind.

简体字	正體字
4-018 先诸王所起平等功德处 谓天神庙堂愿如本修理	4-018 先諸王所起平等功德處 謂天神廟堂願如本修理
4-019a 离杀常行善持戒爱容旧 巧增财无諍勤力恒修善	4-019a 離殺常行善持戒愛容舊 巧增財無諍勤力恒修善
4-019b 清净无积聚不舍于他事 安立为导首受彼功德藏	4-019b 清淨無積聚不捨於他事 安立為導首受彼功德藏
4-020 盲病根不具可悲匄无依 于庙不得遮平等与彼食	4-020 盲病根不具可悲匄無依 於廟不得遮平等與彼食
4-021 道德无求人或住馀王界 供事亦相似应作无此彼	4-021 道德無求人或住餘王界 供事亦相似應作無此彼
4-022 于一切法事应立勤力人 无贪聪智善不侵法畏罪	4-022 於一切法事應立勤力人 無貪聰智善不侵法畏罪

3. On Correct Governance Policies
a. On Maintenance of Pre-Existing Merit-Generating Establishments
018
As for places constructed by the former kings
As merit-generating locations equally available to all,
Namely those temples and halls honoring deities and spirits,
One prays they will be maintained in their original condition.

b. On the Character of Stewards of Such Establishments
019a
Their stewards should abandon killing, always practice goodness,
Uphold morality, be fondly inclusive of those who have long visited,
Skillfully foster increase of assets, remain free of contentiousness,
And be vigorous in constantly cultivating what is good.[120]

019b
They must be devoted to purity, free of personal hoarding,
And vigilant in preventing loss of assets to unrelated endeavors.
Such people should be appointed to serve there as leaders,
Taking in the funds for merit-generation kept in their treasuries.

c. On Fairness in Attendance and in Distribution of Food
020
The blind, the sick, those with disabilities,
The pitiable, beggars, and those with no one to rely on—
They must not be blocked from coming to the temples.
There must be uniform equality in providing them with food.

d. On Fairness in Bestowing Offerings on Practitioners of the Path
021
Those with Path-concordant virtues who may seek nothing at all,
Even though residing in another king's realm,
Should be treated equally in bestowing offerings,
Regardless of whether they abide here or there.

e. On the Character of Those Facilitating Dharma-Related Endeavors
022
In all matters associated with the Dharma,
One should delegate responsibility to vigorous persons
Free of covetousness, intelligent, wise, devoted to goodness,
Not intrusive in the domain of Dharma, and fearful of misdeeds.

简体字	正體字
4-023a 了正论行善亲爱四观净 美语不怯弱上姓能持戒	4-023a 了正論行善親愛四觀淨 美語不怯弱上姓能持戒
4-023b 识恩知他苦如理巧决断 八人互相羞为国立八座	4-023b 識恩知他苦如理巧決斷 八人互相羞為國立八座
4-024a 柔和有大度胆勇甚爱王 坚实能用财无放逸恒善	4-024a 柔和有大度膽勇甚愛王 堅實能用財無放逸恒善
4-024b 熟思所作事能别十二轮 [9]常行四方便应立为大臣	4-024b 熟思所作事能別十二輪 [9]常行四方便應立為大臣
4-025a 持法戒清净了事有干用 能生长护财解义巧书算	4-025a 持法戒清淨了事有幹用 能生長護財解義巧書算
4-025b 于他心事等畏罪亲爱王 富财多眷属宜立为职掌	4-025b 於他心事等畏罪親愛王 富財多眷屬宜立為職掌
4-026 [10]月月应问彼一切财出入 问己法事等喜心善教诲	4-026 [10]月月應問彼一切財出入 問己法事等喜心善教誨

f. On Character and Competence of Ministers, Officials, and Such

023a
[Officials must] comprehend right discourse, act from goodness,
Behave congenially, maintain purity from all four standpoints,[121]
Speak with eloquence, remain invulnerable to timidity,
Be of superior lineage, and be able to uphold moral strictures.

023b
[They should] have a sense of gratitude, be aware of others' hardship,
And be skillful in making judgments founded on right principles.
Find eight such people inclined toward mutual humility and,
For the sake of the country, appoint them to eight cabinet positions.[122]

024a
Those who are gentle, of magnanimous character,
Brave, extremely fond of the King,
Solid in their truthfulness, able to use wealth wisely,
Free of any tendency to be negligent, and constant in goodness—

024b
If they thoroughly contemplate endeavors to be undertaken,
Are able to make distinctions regarding the twelve-part cycle,
And will constantly utilize the four types of skillful means—
People such as these should be appointed as high officials.[123]

g. On Character, Competencies, and Treatment of Financial Officials

025a
Those who uphold the Dharma, observe moral precepts purely,
Understand how things are done, possess extraordinary talent,
Are able to raise funds and protect wealth,
Know what is right, and are skilled in accounting and calculations—

025b
If they are fair in dealing with others,
Are fearful of committing misdeeds, are personally fond of the King,
And if they are already wealthy and have a large retinue—
It is fitting that such people be appointed to governance.

026
They should be questioned each month
Regarding the income and outflow of all their forms of wealth.
Query them as well about their own Dharma works and such.
Then, responding with delighted attitude, skillfully instruct them.

4-027
为法处王位不求名欲尘
王位胜有利异此则不如

4-028
大王即世间多互相食噉
立法王位义汝谛听我说

4-029
长老于王处上族解是非
畏恶多相顺愿彼看王事

4-030
罚系鞭杖等若彼依理行
王恒润大悲[1]于彼更施恩

4-031
为利一切人应恒起慈心
若彼最重恶亦应生大悲

4-032
重恶极害心必于彼行悲
彼即是悲器正行人[2]悲境

4-027
為法處王位不求名欲塵
王位勝有利異此則不如

4-028
大王即世間多互相食噉
立法王位義汝諦聽我說

4-029
長老於王處上族解是非
畏惡多相順願彼看王事

4-030
罰繫鞭杖等若彼依理行
王恒潤大悲[1]於彼更施恩

4-031
為利一切人應恒起慈心
若彼最重惡亦應生大悲

4-032
重惡極害心必於彼行悲
彼即是悲器正行人[2]悲境

简体字　　　　　　正體字

4. On Correct Motivation and Actions as King
a. How the Throne May Generate the Most Supreme Benefit

027
Where one serves as the King for the sake of the Dharma
And refrains from seeking fame or the objects of the desires,
The King's throne is supreme in its ability to provide benefit.
If one strays from this, then the result will be misfortune.

b. Dependence of People and King; Establishing Both dharma and Throne

028
The Great King's close relationship with the people of the world
Is one wherein each generally looks to the other for sustenance.
Here follow principles for establishing both Dharma and throne.
Listen attentively as I explain them for you.

c. Those Whom the King Should Entrust with Oversight of His Affairs

029
Those who are senior in station and older than the King,
Who are of superior family and distinguish right and wrong,
Who fear doing what is bad and are generally agreeable—
One prays they will be appointed to watch over the King's affairs.

d. On Judicious Kindness and Compassion toward Detainees
1) Those Who Have Been Sentenced to Restraints or Flogging

030
Where sentences call for punishment such as restraints or flogging,
Even if those sentences were rightfully ordered,
The King's constant mitigation with the great compassion
Should be even more inclined to bestow kindness on those cases.

2) On the Need for Compassion Even Toward the Extremely Evil

031
For the sake of benefiting all people,
One should constantly draw upon a mind imbued with kindness.
Even if they have committed the most grave sorts of evil,
One should nonetheless raise forth the great compassion.

032
Though the gravely evil possess extremely injurious minds,
One must definitely be compassionate in dealing with their cases.
It is they who are the vessels appropriate for receiving compassion.
Followers of right practice find them suitable objects of compassion.

4-033
贫人若被驻五日须放散
馀人亦如理随一莫拘留

4-034
若于一人所起长系驻心
随人生不护因此恶恒流

4-035
乃至彼未散虽系亦安乐
[3]庄饰浣饮食药扇等相应

4-036
王欲他成器依悲立善教
善恶人皆同不由瞋及欲

4-037
熟思实知已人增起反逆
不杀不逼彼愿王摈他土

4-038
看自家如怨由参人净眼
恒念无放逸愿作如法事

简体字

4-033
貧人若被駐五日須放散
餘人亦如理隨一莫拘留

4-034
若於一人所起長繫駐心
隨人生不護因此惡恒流

4-035
乃至彼未散雖繫亦安樂
[3]莊飾浣飲食藥扇等相應

4-036
王欲他成器依悲立善教
善惡人皆同不由瞋及欲

4-037
熟思實知已人增起反逆
不殺不逼彼願王擯他土

4-038
看自家如怨由參人淨眼
恒念無放逸願作如法事

正體字

3) On Limiting Length of Detention, Especially as Regards the Poor
033
In cases where the poor have been subjected to detention,
[For minor offenses], they must be released within five days.
For all the others as well, they must be dealt with rightfully.
No matter what the case, one must not confine anyone indefinitely.

4) On Negative Effects of Indefinite Detention and Ignoring Rights
034
If, in regard to any single person's case,
One might think they should be kept in long-term detention,
In each such case where one decides not to protect their interests,
Evil will then constantly flow forth due to this very case.[124]

5) On Providing Basic Comforts to Prisoners
035
During that time when they have not yet been released,
Though detained, they should still be allowed happiness.
This extends even to issues of dress, bathing, drink, food,
Medicine, fans, and related concerns.

6) On Compassion and Bias-Free Attitude toward Good and Evil Detainees
036
As the King should wish them to become vessels [of righteousness],
He should institute instruction in goodness based on compassion.
As good and bad people are all to be treated with identical concern,
He should refrain from acting out of animosity or covetousness.

7) For the Incorrigible, Prefer Banishment to Torture or Execution
037
Once one has thoroughly considered and truly knows their cases,
For those persons who increasingly commit grave transgressions,
Still do not put them to death nor subject them to torment.
One prays that the King would rather banish them to other regions.

e. On Security Monitoring of Activities Even of One's Own Clan
038
Watch even your own clan with circumspection due an adversary,
Employing eyes investigating the purity of people's actions.
One must be constantly mindful and free of negligence in this.
One prays such endeavors will be carried out in a lawful manner.[125]

4-039	4-039
赏重加供养有恩人令得 如[4]思德胜负报偿亦如是	賞重加供養有恩人令得 如[4]思德勝負報償亦如是
4-040	4-040
将接为饶花赏施为大果 [5]王树忍辱影民鸟遍依事	將接為饒花賞施為大果 [5]王樹忍辱影民鳥遍依事
4-041	4-041
王持戒能施有威得物心 譬如沙糖丸香[6]刺味相杂	王持戒能施有威得物心 譬如沙糖丸香[6]刺味相雜
4-042	4-042
若王依道理7愚/鱼法则不行 无难无非法恒有法欢乐	若王依道理7愚/魚法則不行 無難無非法恒有法歡樂
4-043	4-043
不从昔世引不可将入来 王位从法得为位莫坏法	不從昔世引不可將入來 王位從法得為位莫壞法
4-044	4-044
王位如肆家8若/苦传如所价 为不更求得此用汝应行	王位如肆家8若/苦傳如所價 為不更求得此用汝應行

简体字　　　　　　　　　正體字

Chapter 4: *Guidance Especially for Rulers*

f. On Commending Meritorious Service

039
Repeatedly bestow gifts commending meritorious service,
Ordering that those demonstrating kindness shall receive them.
Base this on evaluating the superiority of meritorious qualities,
Making the rewards presented be commensurate with that.

g. The Ruler's Giving Rewards: Like a Fruit-Bearing Shade Tree and Birds

040
Escorting off and welcoming back are blossoms of beneficence.
Bestowals of rewards in commendation are its great fruits.
If the royal tree casts the shade of forbearance,
Then the people, like birds, will all flock there, rendering service.

5. Personal Practices Affecting Governance
a. Morality, Giving, and Majesty, Like a Uniquely Flavorful Confection

041
If the King upholds moral virtue, is able to practice giving,
And projects awe-inspiring majesty, he is favored by his subjects
Like a granular-sugar confection
Yielding pungent fragrance and flavor in a pleasing mutual blend.

b. The Importance of Remaining Grounded in Path-Concordant Principles

042
If the King relies on Path-concordant principles,
Then the dharma of "[the big fish eats the little] fish" won't ensue.[126]
Being thus free of difficulties or actions contradicting Dharma,
He will always possess the joy and bliss arising from the Dharma.

c. The Fragility of the Throne and Its Basis in Dharma

043
It is not something brought forth from a previous life,
Nor is it something one can take on to the future life.
As the King's throne is gained by way of the Dharma,
So as to preserve that position, one must not violate the Dharma.[127]

d. Kingship Like a Merchant Dealing in Either Suffering or Royal Privilege

044
Comparing the King's throne to the business of a merchant,
It could be suffering becomes the commodity in which one deals.[128]
To avoid the likelihood of having to continually undergo yet more,
You must carry forth with these correct uses of this position.

简体字	正體字
4-045 王位如肆家王传如所价 为欲更求得此用应修行	4-045 王位如肆家王傳如所價 為欲更求得此用應修行
4-046 转轮王得地或具四天下 但身心二乐馀富贵皆虚	4-046 轉輪王得地或具四天下 但身心二樂餘富貴皆虛
4-047 但对治众苦谓身喜乐受 心乐是想类皆分别所作	4-047 但對治眾苦謂身喜樂受 心樂是想類皆分別所作
4-048 对治苦为体及分别为类 世间一切乐虚故无真实	4-048 對治苦為體及分別為類 世間一切樂虛故無真實
4-049 洲处土居止坐处及衣等 饮食卧具乘妻象马用一	4-049 洲處土居止坐處及衣等 飲食臥具乘妻象馬用一
4-050 若心随一缘即由彼生乐 馀境非缘故是时虚无用	4-050 若心隨一緣即由彼生樂 餘境非緣故是時虛無用

045
Comparing the King's throne to the business of a merchant,
It could be kingship itself is the commodity in which one deals.
To facilitate one's wish to gain it yet again,
One must cultivate these correct uses of this position.[129]

    6. On Limits and Illusoriness of Available Pleasures at any Given Moment
       a. The Limited Scope of Bliss: Physical and Mental. All Else Is False

046
Although the wheel-turning king's acquisition of territory
May extend to include even the four continents,
Still, there are only the two types of bliss: physical and mental.
Hence all remaining aspects of wealth and noble birth are false.

       b. Physical Bliss Is But Lessened Pain, Mental Bliss Is Merely A Perception

047
It is only through the counteraction of the multitude of sufferings
That one speaks of the pleasurable feelings in physical delights.
As mental bliss belongs to the category of mental perceptions,
It is in every case but a creation of discriminating thought.

       c. This Being So, All Worldly Pleasures Are Devoid of Reality

048
In instances where its essence is but counteraction of suffering,
And also where it is merely in the sphere of discriminations,
All such forms of worldly blisses,
Because inherently false, are devoid of any reality.

       d. Though Possessions Are Multifarious, One Can Focus on Only One Thing

049
One's continent, the land in which one lives, where one resides,
Where one sits, the robe one wears, and so forth—
Also: one's drink, food, bedding, carriage,
Wife, elephants, and horses—one can focus on but a single thing.

050
Since the mind, based on the one objective condition it focuses on,
Just then generates bliss solely from that [single objective condition],
Because the other sense objects aren't just then focused upon,
They are just then mere false [conceptions] devoid of any function.

简体字	正體字
4-051 五根缘五尘若心不分别 虽复得成尘不由此生乐	4-051 五根緣五塵若心不分別 雖復得成塵不由此生樂
4-052 此尘根所缘馀则非能所 故所馀根尘真实无有义	4-052 此塵根所緣餘則非能所 故所餘根塵真實無有義
4-053 此尘根所缘心取过去相 分别起净想于彼生乐受	4-053 此塵根所緣心取過去相 分別起淨想於彼生樂受
4-054 一尘心所缘心尘不同世 既离心非尘离尘亦非心	4-054 一塵心所緣心塵不同世 既離心非塵離塵亦非心
4-055 以父母为因汝说有子生 如此缘眼色说有识等生	4-055 以父母為因汝說有子生 如此緣眼色說有識等生

7. WISDOM-INSTILLING CONTEMPLATIONS REFUTING ALL ASPECTS OF "PLEASURE"
a. WHEN ONE REFRAINS FROM SENSE-OBJECT DISCRIMINATIONS, NO BLISS ARISES
051
As the five sense faculties engage the five sense objects as objective
conditions,
If the mind refrains from discriminations in regard to them,
Then, even though they continue to be available as sense objects,
Still, one does not just then generate any bliss on their account.

b. SENSE FACULTIES AND OBJECTS NOT FOCUSED ON ARE JUST THEN MEANINGLESS
052
When this particular sense object is being taken as an objective condition by its corresponding sense faculty,
Then the other [sense faculties and sense objects] aren't just then
serving in any subjective or objective role.
Therefore, all of the remaining sense faculties and sense objects,
In terms of actual reality, are just then meaningless.

c. MIND SEIZES ON THE PAST, DISCRIMINATES, PERCEIVES, AND IMAGINES "BLISS"
053
When this sense object is focused on by its sense faculty,
The mind then seizes on its particular past characteristics.
It then makes discriminations, calls forth perceptions of loveliness,
And generates blissful feelings associated with that [perception].[130]

d. MIND AS SUBJECT AND SENSE DATUM AS OBJECT EXIST IN DIFFERENT TIMES
054
In this case of the single sense object being taken as an objective condition by the mind,
That [moment of focus on the part of the] mind exists in a different
period of time from the sense object itself.
Since, apart from that [moment of focus on the part of the] mind, that
[sense object] could not qualify as a sense object,
Then, apart from the sense object, that [moment of mental focus]
could not qualify as a [subjectively perceiving] mind, either.

e. REFUTATION OF FALSE CONCEPTIONS REGARDING REALITY OF SENSE EXPERIENCE
055
[Citing it as an analogy], taking the father and the mother as causes,
You state that there then exists a child which is born.
In like fashion, [you state that], based on the taking of the eye and
visual forms as conditions,
One may speak of the production of [eye] consciousness and so forth.

简体字	正體字
4-056 去来世根尘不成由无义 不出二世故现尘根无义	4-056 去來世根塵不成由無義 不出二世故現塵根無義
4-057 如眼见火轮由根[9]到乱故 于现在尘中根缘尘亦尔	4-057 如眼見火輪由根[9]到亂故 於現在塵中根緣塵亦爾
4-058 五根及境界是四大尘类 一一大虚故尘[10]根≠亦不有	4-058 五根及境界是四大塵類 一一大虛故塵[10]根≠亦不有
4-059 若大各离成[11]离薪火应然 若离杂无别[12]体尘亦同此判	4-059 若大各離成[11]離薪火應然 若離雜無別[12]體塵亦同此判
4-060 四大二义虚故不成和同 既实无和同故色尘不成	4-060 四大二義虛故不成和同 既實無和同故色塵不成
4-061 识受想及行[13]一一体不成 不合[14]乘缘生非有故无合	4-061 識受想及行[13]一一體不成 不合[14]乘緣生非有故無合

056
Past and future sense faculties and sense objects
Do not qualify as valid because they are meaningless concepts.
Because they do not go beyond this dependence upon those other
    two periods of time,
Present-moment sense faculties and objects are meaningless concepts.

057
Just as the eye's seeing of a "wheel" in a firebrand's twirling
Occurs through an erroneous perception linked to the sense faculty,
Even so, in the sphere of present-time sense objects,
The sense faculty's engagement with sense objects is the same.[131]

058
The five sense faculties and the corresponding objective sense realms
Are of the class of objects subsumed in the four primary elements.
Because, taken individually, each and every one of the primary elements is itself a false concept,
The sense faculties and sense objects themselves possess no valid
    existence either.[132]

059
If the primary elements each having a separate existence were valid,
Then fire should be able to burn in the absence of any fuel.
If their existence were that of a mixed composite,[133] they would have
    no separate substance of their own.
The sense objects, too, are to be judged from this same perspective.

060
Because these two concepts [imputing "existence" of] the four elements are false,
It is impossible to establish the valid existence of any composite phenomenon involving them.
Since, in reality, there is no such combination which occurs,
Form-aggregate sense objects cannot be established [as existents].

061
In the cases of the aggregates of consciousness, feeling, mental perceptions, and karmic formative factors,
In every case, their substance cannot be established [as existent].
There is no "combining" of them which occurs, for their "arising" is a
    phenomenon dependent upon conditions.
As they do not qualify as existents, no "combining" of them occurs.

4-062
如分别喜乐缘苦对治成
如此所计苦因乐坏故成

4-063
于乐和合爱缘无相则灭
于苦远离贪由此观不生

4-064
若依世言说心为能见者
不然离所见能见不成故

4-065
观行覩世间如[15]幻实不有
无取无分别般涅盘如火

4-066
菩萨见如此于菩提不退
由大悲引故后相续至佛

4-067
诸菩萨修道佛说于大乘
无智憎嫉人自害拨不受

4-068
不识功德失于德起失想
或憎嫉胜利故人谤大乘

简体字

4-062
如分別喜樂緣苦對治成
如此所計苦因樂壞故成

4-063
於樂和合愛緣無相則滅
於苦遠離貪由此觀不生

4-064
若依世言說心為能見者
不然離所見能見不成故

4-065
觀行覩世間如[15]幻實不有
無取無分別般涅槃如火

4-066
菩薩見如此於菩提不退
由大悲引故後相續至佛

4-067
諸菩薩修道佛說於大乘
無智憎嫉人自害撥不受

4-068
不識功德失於德起失想
或憎嫉勝利故人謗大乘

正體字

062
In the same way that discriminations imputing joy and bliss
Occur through taking as their object only counteraction of suffering,
So too, this suffering which is reckoned to exist
Only manifests on account of the fading of bliss.

063
As for the craving for proximity to whatever is blissful,
If one focuses on signlessness, it ceases.
As for the desire for separation from whatever involves suffering,
Spurred by this, one should contemplate non-arising.[134]

064
If one relies on the conventional worldly explanation,
It is the mind which is able to perceive.
This is wrong. In the absence of something perceived,
Something able to perceive is not [validly] established.

065
When, in the practice of contemplation, one sees the world
As like an illusion and as, in reality, not existing,
One ceases grasping, ceases discriminations,
And, like a fire [deprived of fuel], realizes *parinirvāṇa*.

066
The bodhisattva's vision is of this very sort,
Making him irreversibly destined to realize bodhi.
Yet, due to being drawn forth by the great compassion,
He continues on thereafter, all the way to buddhahood.

8. THE GRAVE KARMIC ERROR OF THOSE WHO SLANDER THE GREAT VEHICLE

067
The bodhisattva's cultivation of the Path
Was described by the Buddha in the Great Vehicle teachings.
Those persons devoid of wisdom or possessed by hatefulness
Bring harm to themselves by casting it aside, refusing to accept it.

068
Some may fail to distinguish meritorious qualities and faults.
Some imagine that what is in fact meritorious is possessed of faults,
Yet others feel hatred for its having become dominant.[135]
It is for such reasons that people slander the Great Vehicle.

简体字	正體字
4-069 若知罪损他功德能利益 故说诽谤人不识憎嫉善	4-069 若知罪損他功德能利益 故說誹謗人不識憎嫉善
4-070 由不[16]观自利一味利益他 大乘众德器故谤人灰粉	4-070 由不[16]觀自利一味利益他 大乘眾德器故謗人灰粉
4-071 信人由僻执不信由嫉憎 信人谤尚烧何况瞋妬者	4-071 信人由僻執不信由嫉憎 信人謗尚燒何況瞋妬者
4-072 合毒为治毒如医方所说 苦灭恶亦尔此言何相违	4-072 合毒為治毒如醫方所說 苦滅惡亦爾此言何相違
4-073 诸法心先行以心为上首 以苦灭他恶善心人何过	4-073 諸法心先行以心為上首 以苦滅他惡善心人何過
4-074 苦[1]来若能利应取何况乐 或于自及他此是本₂首/萱法	4-074 苦[1]來若能利應取何況樂 或於自及他此是本₂首/萱法
4-075 由能弃小乐后若见大乐 智人舍小乐观于后大乐	4-075 由能棄小樂後若見大樂 智人捨小樂觀於後大樂

069

If they realize that karmic offenses are what bring harm to others
And know meritorious deeds are those able to bring about benefit,
One can only say of those engaging in such slanders
That they are oblivious to the distinction and hence hate the good.

070

Because its proponents disregard their own welfare
Considering it to be of a single flavor with benefiting others,
The Great Vehicle is a repository of manifold meritorious qualities.
Hence its slanderers are bound to be reduced to coals and ashes.

071

For those with faith, it may be due to seizing on the unorthodox.
For those who have no faith, it may be due to hatefulness.
But even the faithful, through slanders, may be destined to burn.
How much more true is this of those compelled by hatred or envy?

9. ON THE DEFENSIBILITY OF ENDURING SUFFERINGS IN SPIRITUAL CULTIVATION

072

Mixing together toxic ingredients for the sake of treating poisoning
Accords with the discourses on medical formulae.
Suffering's role in the cessation of evil is just the same.
How could this statement be considered contradictory?

073

In all dharmas, it is the mind which acts first,
Because it is the mind which serves as one's primary guide.
As for using suffering in causing cessation of other evils—
If done by those devoted to goodness, what fault is there in this?

074

If involvement in some suffering may be beneficial,
One should choose it. How much the more so if bliss is the option?
In a circumstance where benefit may accrue to both self and other,
This action is [verified as right by] the dharma of the ancients.[136]

075

In a case where, from being able to dispense with minor pleasure,
One would later be able to experience great happiness,
The wise would relinquish the [current] minor pleasure
Through contemplating the great happiness bound to follow.

4-076
若不忍此言医师施苦乐/药
犯罪不可恕故汝义不然

4-077
或见事不宜智者由义行
或制或开许此义处处有

4-078
诸菩萨威仪悲为先智成
大乘说如此何因可诽谤

4-079
无知故沈没上乘广深义
故诽谤大乘成自他怨家

4-080
施戒忍精进定智悲为体
佛说大乘尔有何邪说漏

4-081
由施戒利他忍进为自利
定慧脱自他略摄大乘义

4-082
略说佛正教谓解脱自他
此六度为藏何人能拨此

简体字

4-076
若不忍此言醫師施苦樂/藥
犯罪不可恕故汝義不然

4-077
或見事不宜智者由義行
或制或開許此義處處有

4-078
諸菩薩威儀悲為先智成
大乘說如此何因可誹謗

4-079
無知故沈沒上乘廣深義
故誹謗大乘成自他怨家

4-080
施戒忍精進定智悲為體
佛說大乘爾有何邪說漏

4-081
由施戒利他忍進為自利
定慧脫自他略攝大乘義

4-082
略說佛正教謂解脫自他
此六度為藏何人能撥此

正體字

076
If one cannot bear these words,
Then even the physician's dispensing of bitter medicines[137]
Should be deemed an unforgivable crime.
Therefore your ideas on this matter are invalid.[138]

10. On the Great Vehicle's Nature and the Unjustifiability of Disparaging It

077
One may come upon circumstances one views as unfitting.
Here the wise rely on right principle to guide the course of actions,
In some cases exercising restraint, in others allowing exceptions.
This principle is found again and again [in scripture].

078
In the actions associated with a bodhisattva's deportment,
Compassion takes precedence and wisdom ensures their perfection.
As for the Great Vehicle's explanations of this sort—
On what basis could they be disparaged?

079
Through ignorance, one may sink into bewilderment
On meeting the vast and deep meaning of the Supreme Vehicle,[139]
Therefore disparaging the Great Vehicle
And becoming the adversary of both self and others.

080
Giving, moral virtue, patience, vigor,
Meditative discipline, wisdom and compassion form its substance.
The Buddha proclaimed the Great Vehicle as being precisely that.
What errors does it possess that one might claim it has omissions?

081
It is through giving and moral virtue that one benefits others
And through patience and vigor that one benefits self.
Meditative discipline and wisdom liberate both self and others.
This in brief encompasses the meaning of the Great Vehicle.

082
To state it in brief, the authentic teachings of the Buddha
Are held to be those producing liberation of both self and others.
These six perfections are the repository containing them.
Hence who could deny the validity of these?

4-083
福慧为种类佛说菩提道
立此名大乘痴盲不能忍

4-084
如空难思量福慧行成故
诸佛德难思于大乘愿忍

4-085
大德舍利弗佛戒非其境
故佛德难思云何不可忍

4-086
于大乘无生[3]小乘说空灭
无生灭一体自义莫违反

4-087
真空及佛德若如法简择
大小两乘教于智人何诤

4-088
佛不了义说非下人易解
一三乘说中护自体莫伤

4-089
若舍无非福若憎恶无善
若欲爱自身大乘不应谤

简体字

4-083
福慧為種類佛說菩提道
立此名大乘癡盲不能忍

4-084
如空難思量福慧行成故
諸佛德難思於大乘願忍

4-085
大德舍利弗佛戒非其境
故佛德難思云何不可忍

4-086
於大乘無生[3]小乘說空滅
無生滅一體自義莫違反

4-087
真空及佛德若如法簡擇
大小兩乘教於智人何諍

4-088
佛不了義說非下人易解
一三乘說中護自體莫傷

4-089
若捨無非福若憎惡無善
若欲愛自身大乘不應謗

正體字

083
Merit and wisdom are the primary categories of practice
In the path to bodhi proclaimed by the Buddha.
He established this we refer to as the Great Vehicle.
It is such as those blinded by delusion are unable to bear.

084
It is as unfathomable in its vastness as space.
Because they are created through the practice of merit and wisdom,
The meritorious qualities of buddhas are therefore inconceivable.
Thus one prays you will patiently accommodate the Great Vehicle.

085
If for the *ārya*, Śāriputra,
Even the moral virtue of a buddha was beyond his comprehension,
The qualities of a buddha must therefore be inconceivable [as well].
Why then are you unable to acquiesce in this?[140]

086
That which in the Great Vehicle is known as "the unproduced,"
Is described by the Small Vehicle as "cessation via seeing emptiness."
This "unproduced" and this "cessation" are in essence the same.
Their inherent meaning is such as one must not find contradictory.

087
Given that true emptiness and the meritorious qualities of buddhas
Have been correctly analyzed in accordance with Dharma
In the doctrines of both traditions, the Great and Small Vehicles,
What bases for disputation could there be among the wise?

088
Even the Buddha's non-ultimate teachings
Are not such as lesser persons would find easy to comprehend.
As for the contents of the One-Vehicle and Three-Vehicle teachings,
For your own karmic safety, avoid anything which may harm them.[141]

089
In remaining neutral, there is nothing non-meritorious.
Hatefulness, however, is evil and devoid of any good aspects.
Thus if one is inclined to cherish his own personal welfare,
He should refrain from any disparaging of the Great Vehicle.

4-090
菩萨愿及行迴向等彼无
若依小乘修云何成菩萨

4-091
菩萨道四依于小乘不说
何法佛所修而说能胜彼

4-092
约依谛助道佛与彼若同
修因既不异云何果殊越

4-093
菩提行总别小乘中不说
于大乘具辩故智应信受

4-094
如毘伽罗论先教学字母
佛立教如此约受化根[4]性

4-095
有处或说法令彼离众恶
或为成福德或具依前二

4-096
或为遣此二甚深怖劣人
或深/空悲为上为他成菩提

简体字

4-090
菩薩願及行迴向等彼無
若依小乘修云何成菩薩

4-091
菩薩道四依於小乘不說
何法佛所修而說能勝彼

4-092
約依諦助道佛與彼若同
修因既不異云何果殊越

4-093
菩提行總別小乘中不說
於大乘具辯故智應信受

4-094
如毘伽羅論先教學字母
佛立教如此約受化根[4]性

4-095
有處或說法令彼離眾惡
或為成福德或具依前二

4-096
或為遣此二甚深怖劣人
或深/空悲為上為他成菩提

正體字

11. FACTORS UNIQUE TO THE GREAT VEHICLE

090
The vows and practices of the bodhisattva,
Dedication of merit and such—they don't exist in those teachings.
Thus, if one were to rely on the Small Vehicle in one's cultivation,
How could one become a bodhisattva?

091
The Bodhisattva Path and its four reliances[142]
Are not described in the Small Vehicle's teachings.
For which of those dharmas cultivated by the Buddha
Might they be better able to explain them than he?

092
As for reliance on the truths and the auxiliary Path factors—[143]
If the Buddha himself had practiced in a way identical to that—
Since the causes he cultivated would then have been no different,
How could those fruits he realized reach so especially far beyond?

093
The general and specific aspects of the practices leading to bodhi
Are not described within the Small Vehicle's teachings.
However, they were completely delineated in the Great Vehicle.
Thus the wise should have faith in them and should accept them.

12. THE BUDDHA'S RATIONALE IN SETTING FORTH DIFFERENT TEACHINGS

094
In works such as the *Vyākaraṇa*,[144]
They first offer instruction in the study of the alphabet.
As the Buddha's establishment of teachings was comparable to this,
He adapted to differing capacities to accept transforming teaching.

095
There were some circumstances where he proclaimed the Dharma
So that others would abandon the many forms of evil.
In some cases he did so to inspire the creation of merit,
And in still other cases he did so to accomplish both priorities.

096
In some cases, he did so to banish these duality-based concepts,
Teaching extreme profundities alarming those of inferior capacity.
Sometimes emptiness and compassion were set forth as supreme
To allow others to gain perfect realization of bodhi.[145]

4-097
是故聪明人应舍憎大乘
当起胜信受为得无等觉

4-098
由信受大乘及行大乘教
故成无上道中间种种乐

4-099
施戒及忍辱多为在家说
此法悲为上愿汝修成性

4-100
由世不平等王位若乖法
为好名及法事及出家胜

简体字

4-097
是故聰明人應捨憎大乘
當起勝信受為得無等覺

4-098
由信受大乘及行大乘教
故成無上道中間種種樂

4-099
施戒及忍辱多為在家說
此法悲為上願汝修成性

4-100
由世不平等王位若乖法
為好名及法事及出家勝

正體字

13. CONCLUDING DISCUSSION ON CULTIVATING THE GREAT VEHICLE

097
Therefore the intelligent person
Should relinquish any hostility toward the Great Vehicle.
One ought to generate a supreme degree of faith and acceptance
For the sake of realizing the unequaled enlightenment.

098
Through believing in and accepting the Great Vehicle
And then practicing the teachings of the Great Vehicle,
One thereby perfects the unsurpassed Path,
While enjoying the many varieties of happiness in the interim.

099
Giving, moral virtue, and patience
Were in large part proclaimed for edification of the householder.[146]
In this Dharma, it is compassion which is supreme.
One prays you will so cultivate it that it becomes your very nature.

100
Because of the inequalities existing in the world,
The King's throne could involve actions incompatible with Dharma.
In order to preserve one's fine name as well as the Dharma,
Matters could evolve to where leaving the householder's life is best.

宝行王正论

出家正行品第五

5-001 / (01)
初学出家人敬心修禁戒
于木叉毘尼多学破立义

5-002 / (02)
次起正勤心舍离龟类惑
数有五十七谛听我当说

5-003 / (03)
怪/憎谓心相违恨是结他失
覆恶罪名秘及着恶显善

5-004 / (04)
张他名欺诳谄谓曲心续
嫉于他德忧悋心怖畏舍

5-005 / (05)
无羞及无惭于自他为耻
不下不敬他动乱瞋方便

Chapter Five
On Right Practice for Monastics

V. Chapter 5: On Right Practice for Monastics
   A. The First Priority: Study of the Moral Codes

001 / (01)[147]
The monastic new in his studies
Respectfully cultivates the restrictive prohibitions.
In the Pratimokṣa and the Vinaya,[148]
One extensively studies the infractions to establish their meanings.[149]

   B. Next, Eliminating the Fifty-Seven Coarse Faults
002 / (02)
Next, one resolves on right effort
And so abandons the coarse faults.
These are fifty-seven in number.
Listen attentively as I explain them.[150]

003 / (03)
"Anger" (1-*krodha*)[151] refers to the mind's manifesting of aversion.[152]
"Enmity" (2-*upanāha*) involves reifying the faults of others.
Hiding serious offenses is known as "concealment" (3-*mrakṣa*)
And includes clinging to wrong while appearing to be good.

004 / (04)
Inflating the impressions of others constitutes "deception" (4-*māyā*).
"Deviousness" (5-*śāṭhya*) refers to continual crookedness of mind,
"Jealousy" (6-*īrṣyā*), to distress over the qualities of others,
And "miserliness" (7-*mātsarya*), to the mind's fear of relinquishing.

005 / (05)
An "absence of sense of shame" (8-*ahrīkya*) and "absence of dread of
    blame" (9-*anapatrāpya*)
Refer to the issue of remorsefulness in relation to self and to others.
"Non-humility" (10-*asaṃnati*) is failing to respect others.
"Wrathfulness" (11-*saṃrambha*) is a function of being affected by anger.

5-006 / (06) 醉谓不计他放逸不修善 慢类有七种我今当略说	5-006 / (06) 醉謂不計他放逸不修善 慢類有七種我今當略說
5-007 / (07) 若人起分别从下下等等 从下及等胜说此[5]惑为慢	5-007 / (07) 若人起分別從下下等等 從下及等勝說此[5]惑為慢
5-008 / (07-extra*) 下人计自身[6]不如于等人 说此名下慢由自下等类	5-008 / (07-extra*) 下人計自身[6]不如於等人 說此名下慢由自下等類
5-009 / (008) 下人高自身与胜人平等 此惑名高慢由自高等胜	5-009 / (008) 下人高自身與勝人平等 此惑名高慢由自高等勝
5-010 / (09) 下人计自己胜于胜类人 说此名过慢如痈上起泡	5-010 / (09) 下人計自己勝於勝類人 說此名過慢如癰上起泡
5-011 / (10) 于五种取阴自性空无人 由痴故计我说此名我慢	5-011 / (10) 於五種取陰自性空無人 由癡故計我說此名我慢
5-012 / (11ab) 实未得圣道计自身已得 由修偏道故说名增上慢	5-012 / (11ab) 實未得聖道計自身已得 由修偏道故說名增上慢
5-013 / (11cd) 若人由作恶而计自身胜 兼复拨他德说此名邪慢	5-013 / (11cd) 若人由作惡而計自身勝 兼復撥他德說此名邪慢

简体字　　　　　　　　　　正體字

Chapter 5: *On Right Practice for Monastics*

006 / (06)

"[Self]-infatuation" (12-*mada*) refers to taking no account of others.[153]
"Negligence" (13-*pramāda*) refers to failing to cultivate good qualities.
"Arrogance" (*māna*) is of seven types[154]
I shall now briefly describe them.

007 / (07)

If a person initiates discriminations
By which he imputes to himself relative inferiority or equality,
Or, if he assumes superiority where he is only an inferior or equal,
These faults are collectively referred to as: "arrogance" (14-*māna*).

008 / (07-extra*)

When a relatively inferior person reckons with regard to himself
That he is not comparable to a person actually his equal,
This constitutes [outward] "arrogance in inferiority" (*adhamo māna*).
It stems from rating oneself as inferior to those one's equal.[155]

009 / (08)

When a relatively inferior person elevates his self-estimation,
Thus claiming equality with a person who is his own superior,
This fault is known as "elevating arrogance" (15-*atimāna*).
It stems from elevating oneself to equality with superior persons.

010 / (09)

When a relatively inferior person reckons that he himself
Is superior to persons who are actually his own superiors,
This is known as "over-reaching arrogance" (16-*māna-atimāna*).
It is compared to developing a pustule on top of an abscess.

011 / (10)

As regards the five appropriated aggregates (*upādāna-skandha*),[156]
They are empty of inherent existence and devoid of any "person."
When, because of delusion, one imputes existence of "self" therein,
This is known as "self-imputing arrogance" (17-*asmi-māna*).

012 / (11ab)

When in fact one has not yet realized the path of the Āryas,
Yet one nonetheless reckons that he has achieved such realizations,
This stems from cultivating a skewed path.
This is known as "overweening arrogance" (18-*abhi-māna*).

013 / (11cd)

If a person, on account of having committed some evil,
Thereby reckons himself to be superior,
While simultaneously brushing aside the virtues of others,
This is what is known as "perverse arrogance" (19-*mithyā-māna*).

简体字	正體字
5-014 / (12) 我今无复用或能下自体 此亦名下慢但缘自体起	5-014 / (12) 我今無復用或能下自體 此亦名下慢但緣自體起
5-015 / (13ab) 为求利养赞故守摄六根 能隐贪欲意此惑名贡高	5-015 / (13ab) 為求利養讚故守攝六根 能隱貪欲意此惑名貢高
5-016 / (13cd) 为得利供养于他起爱语 此惑缘世法说此名谢言	5-016 / (13cd) 為得利供養於他起愛語 此惑緣世法說此名謝言
5-017 / (14ab) 为欲得彼物若赞美此财 说名为现相能示自心故	5-017 / (14ab) 為欲得彼物若讚美此財 說名為現相能示自心故
5-018 / (14cd) 为欲得所求现前非拨他 说名为诃责能伏彼令顺	5-018 / (14cd) 為欲得所求現前非撥他 說名為訶責能伏彼令順
5-019 / (15ab) 由施欲求利或赞彼先德 说名利求利此五邪命摄	5-019 / (15ab) 由施欲求利或讚彼先德 說名利求利此五邪命攝
5-020 / (15cd) 若人缘他失心数种种诵 说名为憎嗌此或习恨心	5-020 / (15cd) 若人緣他失心數種種誦 說名為憎嗌此或習恨心

014 / (12)

[If one thinks], "I am now of no further use,"
Or becomes otherwise able to demote himself,
This, too, is [inward] "arrogance in inferiority" (20-*adhamo-māna*).
This type takes only oneself as the object occasioning its arising.[157]

015 / (13ab)

When, for the sake of seeking beneficial offerings and praise,
One carefully monitors and controls the six sense faculties,
Thus enabling oneself to hide his covetousness-based intentions,
This constitutes a fault known as "hypocrisy" (21-*kuhanā*).

016 / (13cd)

When, for the sake of obtaining beneficial offerings,
One speaks in a manner intended to please someone,
This is a fault which takes worldly dharmas as its object.
This constitutes what is known as "flattery" (22-*lapanā*).

017 / (14ab)

When, for the sake of obtaining something owned by another,
One praises and admires the beauty of such valuables,
This is known as "hinting" (23-*naimittikatva*).
Because it is able to reveal one's thoughts to others.

018 / (14cd)

When, for the sake of obtaining something one seeks,
One stirs up someone through confrontational criticism,
This is known as "coercion through reproval" (24-*naiṣpeṣikatvam*),
It is able to induce submissiveness and cause compliance.[158]

019 / (15ab)

When one seeks gains from making gifts
Or else from praising another's prior meritorious behavior,
This is known as "seeking gains from gains" (25-*lābhena lipsā lābhānā*).
This is included among the five sorts of wrong livelihoods.

020 / (15cd)

If a person, taking the faults of others as the focus,
In all manner of ways, repeatedly recites them in his own mind,
This is known as "quiet condemnation" (26-*).
This may involve a mind prone to habitual animosity.[159]

5-021 / (16)
惊怖不能安由无知及病
于下尵自具毁甾及懈着

5-022 / (17)
欲瞋痴污想说名种种相/想
不如现观察说名非思惟

5-023 / (18)
于正事懈怠说名不恭敬
于师无尊心说名不尊重

5-024 / (19)
上心欲所起于外名坚着
上心坚欲生最重名遍着

5-025 / (20)
自财生长欲无足心名贪
爱着于他物是名不等欲

5-026 / (21)
于非境女人求得非法欲
自无德显德说名为恶欲

5-027 / (22)
离知足恒求说此名大欲
愿他知我德说名为识欲

简体字

5-021 / (16)
驚怖不能安由無知及病
於下尵自具毀甾及懈著

5-022 / (17)
欲瞋癡污想說名種種相/想
不如現觀察說名非思惟

5-023 / (18)
於正事懈怠說名不恭敬
於師無尊心說名不尊重

5-024 / (19)
上心欲所起於外名堅著
上心堅欲生最重名遍著

5-025 / (20)
自財生長欲無足心名貪
愛著於他物是名不等欲

5-026 / (21)
於非境女人求得非法欲
自無德顯德說名為惡欲

5-027 / (22)
離知足恒求說此名大欲
願他知我德說名為識欲

正體字

Chapter 5: *On Right Practice for Monastics*

021 / (16)

"Immobilizing anxiety" (27-*staimitya*) involves inability to be at peace
Caused by ignorance, by illness,
By [realization of one's own] inferior and coarse personal qualities,
By experiencing disparaging denunciation, or by [compulsive] indulgence in indolent attachments.

022 / (17)

In cases where desire, hatred, or delusion pollute one's thinking,
This is known as "multifarious thinking" (28-*nānātva-saṃjñā*).[160]
Where one's observations don't accord with present circumstances,
This is known as "non-reflectiveness" (29-*amanaskāra*).

023 / (18)

When one is lazy as regards matters requiring propriety,
This is known as "disrespectfulness" (30-*).
When one has no thoughts of veneration toward his own gurus,
This is known as "irreverence" (31-*).[161]

024 / (19)

Where generated by dominant thoughts of desire,
And focused outwardly, [the fault] is called "attachment" (32-*gardha*).
Where generated by dominant thoughts of firmly-rooted desire,
When most severe, it is "pervasive attachment" (33-*pari-gardha*).

025 / (20)

When one's own wealth generates and increases desire [for more]
And involves an insatiable mind, this is termed "avarice" (34-*lobha*).
When one craves and becomes attached to the possessions of others,
This is known as "inordinate avarice" (35-*viṣamo lobha*).

026 / (21)

When, toward a woman beyond the bounds of propriety,
One seeks to consummate Dharma-contravening desires
And [facilitates it by] feigning virtues, though devoid of virtues,
This is what we term "evil lust" (36-*pāpecchatā*).

027 / (22)

If, abandoning satiability, one constantly indulges covetousness,
This is known as "extreme desire" (37-*mahecchatā*).
When one prays others will become aware of one's qualities,
This is known as "desire for recognition" (38-*icchepsutā*).

简体字	正體字
5-028 / (23) 不能安苦受说名为不忍 于师尊正事邪行名不贵	**5-028 / (23)** 不能安苦受說名為不忍 於師尊正事邪行名不貴
5-029 / (24) 如法善言教轻慢名难语 于亲人爱着思惟名亲觉	**5-029 / (24)** 如法善言教輕慢名難語 於親人愛著思惟名親覺
5-030 / (25) 由欲于方处思得名土觉 不虑死怖畏说名不死觉	**5-030 / (25)** 由欲於方處思得名土覺 不慮死怖畏說名不死覺
5-031 / (26) 由真实功德愿他尊重我 此思缘他识说名顺觉觉	**5-031 / (26)** 由真實功德願他尊重我 此思緣他識說名順覺覺
5-032 / (27) 由爱及憎心思自益损他 缘自及馀人说名害他觉	**5-032 / (27)** 由愛及憎心思自益損他 緣自及餘人說名害他覺
5-033 / (28) 忧忆染污心无依名不安 身沈说名极迟缓名懈怠	**5-033 / (28)** 憂憶染污心無依名不安 身沈說名極遲緩名懈怠

028 / (23)
When one is unable to be at peace with experiencing suffering,
This is known as "non-forbearance" (39-*akṣānti*).
When, as regards right conduct serving gurus or the venerable,
One deviates in one's actions, this is "impropriety" (40-*anācāra*).

029 / (24)
When, reacting to well-phrased Dharma-concordant teaching,
One becomes slighting and arrogant, this is "refractoriness to instruction" (41-*daurvacasya*).
When one cherishes a fondly clinging attachment for relatives
And thinks about them obsessively, this is "kinship ideation" (42-*jñāti-saṃbandho-vitarka*).

030 / (25)
When, on account of a desire to reside in another location,
One ponders how that would be, this is "region-related ideation" (43-*jānapada-vitarka*).
When one doesn't entertain any thoughts apprehensive of death,
This is known as "immortality ideation" (44-*amara-vitarka*).

031 / (26)
When, based on the possession of actual meritorious qualities,
One prays that others will revere him,
This strain of thought which takes others' recognition as the object
Is known as "recognition-dependent ideation" (45-*anu-vijñapti-saṃyukto-vitarka*).

032 / (27)
When, because of thoughts devoted to love and disdain,
One ruminates on self-benefit and harm to others,
Taking as the objective condition "self" and "others,"
This is what we term "harmful ideation" (46-*vihiṃsā-vitarka*).

033 / (28)
Where the mind is sullied through troubling over recollections
But there is no justification for it, this is known as "uneasiness" (47-*arati*).
When physical vitality seems sunken away, this is "exhaustion" (48-*tandrā*).
Proceeding only with slowness is known as "indolence" (49-*ālasya*).

简体字	正體字
5-034 / (29) 由随上心惑曲发身名频 身乱不节食说名为食醉	5-034 / (29) 由隨上心惑曲發身名頻 身亂不節食說名為食醉
5-035 / (30) 身心极疲羸说名为下劣 贪爱于五尘说名为欲欲	5-035 / (30) 身心極疲羸說名為下劣 貪愛於五塵說名為欲欲
5-036 / (31) 于他损害意从九因缘生 三时疑灾横说名为瞋恚	5-036 / (31) 於他損害意從九因緣生 三時疑災橫說名為瞋恚
5-037 / (32) 由身心重故事无能名弱 心晦说名睡身心掉名动	5-037 / (32) 由身心重故事無能名弱 心晦說名睡身心掉名動
5-038 / (33) 由恶事生悔忧后燋然名 于三宝四谛犹豫说名疑	5-038 / (33) 由惡事生悔憂後燋然名 於三寶四諦猶豫說名疑
5-039 / (34) 若出家菩萨须离此麁类 若能免此恶对治德易生	5-039 / (34) 若出家菩薩須離此麁類 若能免此惡對治德易生

034 / (29)

When, on account of coursing in dominant deluded thought,
One adopts skewed physical mannerisms [such as scowling], this is
   "distorted physical expression" (50-*vijṛmbhikā*).
When, as a function of a disorderly approach to physical discipline,
   one fails to regulate eating,
This is known as "food intoxication" (51-*bhakta-sammada*).

035 / (30)

When body and mind manifest extreme weariness and weakness,
This is known as "mental depression" (52-*ceto-līnatvam*).
When one craves the five sense objects,
This is known as "desire" (53-*kāma-chanda*).[162]

036 / (31)

When one contemplates inflicting harm on another,
This may arise from nine different causes and conditions
Linked to concern over misfortune in any of the three times.[163]
This is known as "ill-will" (54-*vyāpāda*).[164]

037 / (32)

When, on account of the body and mind seeming weighed down,
One is unable to undertake any endeavors, this is "lethargy"
   (55a-*styāna*).[165]
When mental clarity becomes murky, this is "drowsiness"
   (55b-*middha*).
When body and mind are stirred up, this is "excitedness"
   (56a-*auddhatya*).[166]

038 / (33)

On account of evil deeds, one generates "regretfulness" (56b-*kaukṛtya*),
So-named on account of anguish over what will come later.
When with respect to the Three Jewels and the four truths,
One experiences hesitancy, this is known as "doubtfulness"
   (57-*vicikitsā*).[167]

039 / (34)

If one is a monastic bodhisattva,
He must abandon such coarse factors as these.
If one is able to avoid these evils,
Having counteracted them, meritorious qualities then easily arise.

简体字	正體字
5-040 / (35) 此中诸功德菩萨应修治 谓施戒及忍勤定慧悲等	5-040 / (35) 此中諸功德菩薩應修治 謂施戒及忍勤定慧悲等
5-041 / (36) 舍自物名施起利他名戒 解脱瞋名忍摄善名精进	5-041 / (36) 捨自物名施起利他名戒 解脱瞋名忍攝善名精進
5-042 / (37) 心寂静名定通真义名智 于一切众生一味利名悲	5-042 / (37) 心寂靜名定通真義名智 於一切眾生一味利名悲
5-043 / (38) 施生富戒乐忍爱勤焰炽 定静智解脱悲生一切利	5-043 / (38) 施生富戒樂忍愛勤焰熾 定靜智解脱悲生一切利
5-044 / (39) 此七法若成俱得至究竟 难思智境界₁今/令到世尊位	5-044 / (39) 此七法若成俱得至究竟 難思智境界₁今/令到世尊位
5-045 / (40) 如于小乘中说诸声闻地 于大乘亦尔说菩萨十地	5-045 / (40) 如於小乘中說諸聲聞地 於大乘亦爾說菩薩十地
5-046 / (41) 初地名欢喜于中喜希有 由三结灭尽及生在佛家	5-046 / (41) 初地名歡喜於中喜希有 由三結滅盡及生在佛家

C. Additional Practices: The Perfections, Compassion, and Related Dharmas

040 / (35)
All of the meritorious qualities described herein
Are such as the bodhisattva should cultivate.
Specifically, they are giving, moral virtue, and patience,
Vigor, meditative discipline, wisdom, compassion, and the rest.

1. The Perfections and Compassion

041 / (36)
"Giving" is the relinquishing of one's own possessions.
"Moral virtue" involves promoting the benefit of others.
"Patience" is liberating oneself from hatefulness.
"Vigor" is the focused cultivation of goodness.

042 / (37)
"Meditative discipline" involves bringing the mind to stillness.
"Wisdom" is the comprehension of the genuine meaning.
When the nature of one's relationship to all beings
Is a singular flavor of concern for their benefit, this is "compassion."

043 / (38)
"Giving" generates wealth and "moral virtue" brings happiness.
"Patience" brings beauty and "vigor" generates flaming intensity.
"Meditation" brings stillness and "wisdom" generates liberation.
"Compassion" produces every type of benefit.

044 / (39)
These seven dharmas, if perfected,
Collectively bring about realization of the ultimate,
The realm of inconceivable wisdom,
And cause one to reach the Bhagavān's position.[168]

2. On the Ten Bodhisattva Grounds

045 / (40)
Just as in the Small Vehicle
Wherein one speaks of the stations of the Śrāvaka disciples,
So, too, it is in the Great Vehicle
Wherein the "ten grounds" of the Bodhisattvas are described.

a. The First Ground: The Ground of Joyfulness

046 / (41)
The first of the grounds is known as "the ground of joyfulness."[169]
In it, one experiences rare joy
Arising due to the utter destruction of the three fetters
And due to being born into the family of the Buddhas.

简体字	正體字
5-047 / (42-1*) 因此地果报现前修施度 于百佛世界不动得自在	5-047 / (42-1*) 因此地果報現前修施度 於百佛世界不動得自在
5-048 / (42-2*) 于剡浮等洲为大转轮王 于世间恒转宝轮及法轮	5-048 / (42-2*) 於剡浮等洲為大轉輪王 於世間恒轉寶輪及法輪
5-049 / (43) 第二名无垢身口意等业 十种皆清净自性得自在	5-049 / (43) 第二名無垢身口意等業 十種皆清淨自性得自在
5-050 / (44-1*) 因此地果报现前修戒度 于千佛世界不动得自在	5-050 / (44-1*) 因此地果報現前修戒度 於千佛世界不動得自在
5-051 / (44-2*) 仙人天帝释能除天爱欲 天魔及外道皆所不能动	5-051 / (44-2*) 仙人天帝釋能除天愛欲 天魔及外道皆所不能動
5-052 / (45) 第三名明焰寂慧光明生 由定及神通欲瞋惑灭故	5-052 / (45) 第三名明焰寂慧光明生 由定及神通欲瞋惑滅故
5-053 / (46-1*) 因此地果报现前修忍[2]辱 于万佛世界不动得自在	5-053 / (46-1*) 因此地果報現前修忍[2]辱 於萬佛世界不動得自在

047 / (42-1*)
On account of the karmic rewards specific to this ground,
Cultivation of the perfection of giving manifests as foremost.
In the worlds of a hundred buddhas,
One becomes unshakable and gains sovereign independence.[170]

048 / (42-2*)
Reigning over Jambudvīpa and the other continents,
One becomes a wheel-turning universal monarch
Who constantly sets turning in the world
His precious wheel and the wheel of the Dharma.

b. THE SECOND GROUND: THE GROUND OF NON-DEFILEMENT
049 / (43)
The second is named "the ground of stainlessness."[171]
In it, the karma of the body, mouth, and mind,
In all of its ten different types, becomes entirely pure.[172]
One becomes, by one's very nature, sovereignly independent.

050 / (44-1*)
On account of the karmic rewards specific to this ground,
Cultivation of the perfection of moral virtue manifests as foremost.
In the worlds of a thousand buddhas,
One becomes unshakable and gains sovereign independence.

051 / (44-2*)
[One may manifest] as a rishi or as Śakra Devānām Indra,
With the ability to rid oneself of the desires of the gods.
One becomes such as the heavenly demons and non-Buddhists
Are all entirely unable to move.

c. THE THIRD GROUND: THE GROUND OF ILLUMINATION
052 / (45)
The third is named "the ground of illumination"
Where one generates the brilliant light of quiescent wisdom.[173]
Through meditative absorption and spiritual powers,
One destroys the delusions associated with desire and hatred.

053 / (46-1*)
On account of the karmic rewards specific to this ground,
Cultivation of the perfection of patience manifests as foremost.
In the worlds of a myriad buddhas,
One becomes unshakable and gains sovereign independence.

简体字	正體字
5-054 / (46-2*) [3]作夜摩天帝灭身见习气 一切邪师执能破能正教	5-054 / (46-2*) [3]作夜摩天帝滅身見習氣 一切邪師執能破能正教
5-055 / (47-1*) 第四名烧然智火光焰生 因此地果报精进度现前	5-055 / (47-1*) 第四名燒然智火光焰生 因此地果報精進度現前
5-056 / (47-2*) 多修习道品为灭惑生道 兜率陀天主除外道见戒	5-056 / (47-2*) 多修習道品為滅惑生道 兜率陀天主除外道見戒
5-057 / (48*) 由得生自在于十方佛土 往还无障碍馀义如前地	5-057 / (48*) 由得生自在於十方佛土 往還無障礙餘義如前地
5-058 / (49) 第五名难胜魔二乘不及 圣谛微细义证见所生故	5-058 / (49) 第五名難勝魔二乘不及 聖諦微細義證見所生故
5-059 / (50) 因此地果报定度得现前 为化乐天主迴二乘向大	5-059 / (50) 因此地果報定度得現前 為化樂天主迴二乘向大
5-060 / (51) 第六名现前正向佛法故 由数习定慧证得灭圆满	5-060 / (51) 第六名現前正向佛法故 由數習定慧證得滅圓滿

054 / (46-2*)
One may manifest as the emperor of the Yāma Heaven,
Destroying the habitual inclination to view the body [as self].
As for the attachments of all teachers of error-ridden traditions,
One is able to refute them and able to set forth correct teachings.

   d. THE FOURTH GROUND: THE GROUND OF FLAMING INTELLIGENCE

055 / (47-1*)
The fourth is named "the ground of flaming [intelligence]."[174]
In it, the flaming light of the fire of wisdom is generated.
On account of the karmic rewards specific to this ground,
Cultivation of the perfection of vigor manifests as foremost.

056 / (47-2*)
One devotes much cultivation to the components of the Path[175]
For the sake of destroying delusions and generating the Path.
One becomes lord over the Tuṣita Heaven
And does away with views and austerities of non-Buddhists.

057 / (48*)
Through gaining sovereign independence in the ability to be born
Throughout the buddhalands of the ten directions,
One comes and goes without obstruction.
The remaining ideas accord with those noted on previous grounds.

   e. THE FIFTH GROUND: THE GROUND OF BEING DIFFICULT TO OVERCOME

058 / (49)
The fifth is "the ground of being difficult to overcome."[176]
Neither demons nor Two-Vehicles advocates can reach it.
As for the extremely subtle meaning of the truths of the Āryas,
It is generated through realized perception.

059 / (50)
On account of the karmic rewards specific to this ground,
Cultivation of the perfection of meditation manifests as foremost.
One becomes the lord of the Creation of Bliss Heaven
And turns Two-Vehicles practitioners toward the Great Vehicle.

   f. THE SIXTH GROUND: THE GROUND OF DIRECT FACING

060 / (51)
The sixth is called "the ground of direct facing"
Because it faces directly toward the Dharma of the Buddha.[177]
Through repeated coursing in meditative absorption and wisdom,
One gains complete realization of cessation.

简体字	正體字
5-061 / (52) 因此地果报般若度现前 他化自在天能教[1]真俗谛	5-061 / (52) 因此地果報般若度現前 他化自在天能教[1]真俗諦
5-062 / (53) 第七名远行远行数相续 于中念念得无生及无灭	5-062 / (53) 第七名遠行遠行數相續 於中念念得無生及無滅
5-063 / (54-1*) 因此地果报方便智现前 得为大梵王能通第一义	5-063 / (54-1*) 因此地果報方便智現前 得為大梵王能通第一義
5-064 / (54-2*) 证方便胜智六度生无间 于三乘世俗为最第一师	5-064 / (54-2*) 證方便勝智六度生無間 於三乘世俗為最第一師
5-065 / (55*) 童子地不动由不出真观 无分别难思非身口意境	5-065 / (55*) 童子地不動由不出真觀 無分別難思非身口意境
5-066 / (56-1*) 因此地果报愿度常现前 胜遍光梵主净土等自在	5-066 / (56-1*) 因此地果報願度常現前 勝遍光梵主淨土等自在
5-067 / (56-2*) 二乘等不及于真俗一义 俱修动静故行二利无[2]间	5-067 / (56-2*) 二乘等不及於真俗一義 俱修動靜故行二利無[2]間

Chapter 5: *On Right Practice for Monastics*

061 / (52)
On account of the karmic rewards specific to this ground,
Cultivation of the perfection of prajñā manifests as foremost.
One abides in the "Free Control of Others' Emanations" Heaven
And is able to teach both the genuine and mundane truths.

> g. THE SEVENTH GROUND: THE GROUND OF BEING FAR-REACHING

062 / (53)
The seventh is "the ground of being far-reaching"
Wherein one travels far, repeatedly, and continuously.[178]
Within it, one realizes in every single thought-moment
The unproduced and the undestroyed.

063 / (54-1*)
On account of the karmic rewards specific to this ground,
The perfections of knowledges and expedients become foremost.
One becomes the king of the Great Brahma Heaven
And becomes able to penetratingly understand the ultimate truth.

064 / (54-2*)
One realizes both expedient and superior forms of wisdom.
The six perfections arise ceaselessly.
As regards the Three Vehicles and mundane aspects of the world,
One manifests as the most supreme of all teachers.

> h. THE EIGHTH GROUND: THE KUMĀRA GROUND, THE GROUND OF IMMOVABILITY

065 / (55*)
On "the ground of virgin youth," one abides in "immovability"
Through never emerging from contemplation of [ultimate] truth.
The absence of discriminations herein is inconceivable
And is a state beyond the realm of body, mouth, and mind.[179]

066 / (56-1*)
On account of the karmic rewards specific to this ground,
Cultivation of the perfection of vows manifests as foremost.
One exceeds lords of Immeasurable Light and Brahma Heavens
And equals those in the purelands in one's enjoyment of sovereign
    independence.

067 / (56-2*)
This is such as practitioners of the Two Vehicles do not reach.
Ultimate truth and worldly truth are of a single meaning.
Through complete cultivation in both movement and stillness,
One carries on ceaselessly with the two types of benefit.[180]

简体字	正體字
5-068 / 57 第九名善慧法王太子位 此中智最胜由通达四辩	5-068 / 57 第九名善慧法王太子位 此中智最勝由通達四辯
5-069 / (58) 因此地果报力度常现前 为遍净梵王四答难无等	5-069 / (58) 因此地果報力度常現前 為遍淨梵王四答難無等
5-070 / (59) 第十名法云能雨正法雨 佛光水灌身受佛灌顶位	5-070 / (59) 第十名法雲能雨正法雨 佛光水灌身受佛灌頂位
5-071 / (60a) 因此地果报智度常现前 为净居梵王大自在天[3]王	5-071 / (60a) 因此地果報智度常現前 為淨居梵王大自在天[3]王
5-072 / (60b) 智慧境难思诸佛秘密藏 得具足自在后生补处位	5-072 / (60b) 智慧境難思諸佛祕密藏 得具足自在後生補處位
5-073 / (61) 如此菩萨地十种我已说 佛地与彼异具胜德难量	5-073 / (61) 如此菩薩地十種我已說 佛地與彼異具勝德難量
5-074 / (62) 此地但略说十力等相应 随此一一力难量如虚空	5-074 / (62) 此地但略說十力等相應 隨此一一力難量如虛空

i. The Ninth Ground: The Ground of Fine Intelligence

068 / (57)

The ninth is known as "the ground of fine intelligence."[181]
It is the position of the crown prince of Dharma.
Herein, one's wisdom becomes the most supreme
Through penetrating realization of the four types of eloquence.[182]

069 / (58)

On account of the karmic rewards specific to this ground,
Cultivation of the powers perfection always manifests as foremost.
One becomes king of Immeasurable Purity and Brahma Heavens
And is unequaled in the four responses to challenging questions.[183]

j. The Tenth Ground: The Ground of the Dharma Cloud

070 / (59)

The tenth is called "the ground of the Dharma cloud."[184]
One is able to let fall the rain of right Dharma.
The waters of Buddha's light pour down on him
And he then assumes the position of one anointed on the crown by the Buddhas.

071 / (60a)

On account of the karmic rewards specific to this ground,
The perfection of knowledges constantly manifests as foremost.
One becomes king of the Pure Dwelling and Brahma heavens
As well as king of the Heaven of Great Sovereign Independence.

072 / (60b)

One's realm of wisdom realization becomes inconceivable,
[Equaling] the secret treasury of the Buddhas' [wisdom].
One gains completely perfected sovereign independence
And then is born into the penultimate position.

3. The Ground of Buddhahood

073 / (61)

The grounds of a bodhisattva such as set forth herein
Are of these ten types I have just now explained.
The ground of buddhahood is distinctly different from them.
In it, one perfects supreme qualities beyond measure.

074 / (62)

This ground is only briefly described herein
As corresponding in attributes to the ten powers and so forth.
In the case of each and every one of these powers,
Its range is as immeasurable as empty space itself.

简体字	正體字
5-075 / (63) 如此等可言诸佛无量德 如十方虚空及地水火风	5-075 / (63) 如此等可言諸佛無量德 如十方虛空及地水火風
5-076 / (64) 诸佛无量德于馀人难信 若不见此因难量如此果	5-076 / (64) 諸佛無量德於餘人難信 若不見此因難量如此果
5-077 / (65) 为此因及果现前佛支提 日夜各三遍愿诵二十偈	5-077 / (65) 為此因及果現前佛支提 日夜各三遍願誦二十偈
5-078 / (66) 诸佛法及僧一切诸菩萨 我顶礼归依馀可尊亦敬	5-078 / (66) 諸佛法及僧一切諸菩薩 我頂禮歸依餘可尊亦敬
5-079 / (67) 我离一切恶摄持一切善 众生诸善行随喜及顺行	5-079 / (67) 我離一切惡攝持一切善 眾生諸善行隨喜及順行
5-080 / 68 头面礼诸佛合掌劝请住 愿为转法轮穷生死后际	5-080 / 68 頭面禮諸佛合掌勸請住 願為轉法輪窮生死後際
5-081 / (69) 从此行我德已作及未[4]作 因此愿众生皆发菩提心	5-081 / (69) 從此行我德已作及未[4]作 因此願眾生皆發菩提心

075 / (63)
One is able in this manner to attempt a description
Of the countless meritorious qualities of a buddha.
They compare in boundlessness to the ten directions of space,
Including all of the earth, water, fire, and wind therein.

076 / (64)
The incalculably many meritorious qualities of buddhas
Are difficult for others even to believe in.
If one fails to perceive the nature of these causes,
It remains difficult to fathom [such an immeasurable] effect as this.

4. TWENTY VERSES TO GENERATE THE CAUSES AND RESULT OF BUDDHAHOOD
077 / (65)
For the sake of generating these causes as well as their effects,
In the direct presence of a *caitya* dedicated to the Buddhas,
Three times each day and three times each night,
I pray that one will recite these following twenty verses:[185]

078 / (66)
Before the Buddhas, the Dharma, and the Sangha,
And also before all Bodhisattvas,
I bow down in reverence and take refuge in them,
Expressing reverence as well to all others worthy of veneration.

079 / (67)
I hereby abandon every form of evil
And gather in and assimilate every form of goodness.
All of the goodness practiced by beings—
I rejoice in it all, while according with it in my own actions.

080 / (68)
I bow down my head in reverence to the Buddhas,
And, palms together, urge and beseech them to abide among us.
I pray that they shall set in motion the wheel of Dharma,
Even to the very end of all births and deaths throughout the future.

081 / (69)
Whatsoever merit accrues to me from these practices,
Including that already created as well as that not yet created—
Through the power of this, I pray that beings
Shall all generate the mind resolved on realizing bodhi.

简体字	正體字
5-082 / (70) 度一切障难圆满无垢根 具净命相应愿彼自在事	5-082 / (70) 度一切障難圓滿無垢根 具淨命相應願彼自在事
5-083 / (71) 一切具无边与宝手相应 穷后际无尽愿众生如此	5-083 / (71) 一切具無邊與寶手相應 窮後際無盡願眾生如此
5-084 / (72) 愿一切女人皆成胜丈夫 恒于一切时明足得圆满	5-084 / (72) 願一切女人皆成勝丈夫 恒於一切時明足得圓滿
5-085 / (73) 胜形貌威德好色他爱见 无病力[5]办具长寿愿彼然	5-085 / (73) 勝形貌威德好色他愛見 無病力[5]辦具長壽願彼然
5-086 / (74) 解脱诸苦畏一向归三宝 于方便善巧佛法为大财	5-086 / (74) 解脫諸苦畏一向歸三寶 於方便善巧佛法為大財
5-087 / (75) 慈悲喜净舍恒居四梵住 施戒忍精进定智所庄严	5-087 / (75) 慈悲喜淨捨恒居四梵住 施戒忍精進定智所莊嚴
5-088 / (76) 圆满福慧行相好光明照 愿彼难思量行十地无碍	5-088 / (76) 圓滿福慧行相好光明照 願彼難思量行十地無礙
5-089 / (77) 与此德相应馀德所[6]庄严 解脱一切过愿我爱众生	5-089 / (77) 與此德相應餘德所[6]莊嚴 解脫一切過願我愛眾生

Chapter 5: *On Right Practice for Monastics*

082 / (70)
May they overstep the difficulties arising from any obstructions,
Entirely perfect the undefiled faculties,
And accord completely with pure livelihood.
I pray they shall enjoy sovereign independence in their endeavors.

083 / (71)
May they be able to obtain all things without limit,
Just as if they held in their hands a wish-fulfilling jewel.
May this continue endlessly, even to the exhaustion of future time.
I pray that beings will enjoy just such circumstances as these.

084 / (72)
I pray that all women
Will be able to achieve rebirth as the most supreme men[186]
And will constantly forever after
Be able to gain perfect fulfillment in the clarities and bases.[187]

085 / (73)
May beings gain superior stature, countenance, stateliness,
And fine physical features others find pleasing to behold.
Free of sickness, strong, able to carry out endeavors,
And enjoying long lives—I pray their circumstances may be just so.

086 / (74)
May they become liberated from all forms of suffering and fear,
At all points along the way take the Refuges in the Three Jewels,
And find the expedients and fine skillful means
Within the Buddha's Dharma to be for them great wealth.[188]

087 / (75)
Kindness, compassion, sympathetic joy, and pure equanimity—
May they constantly abide in these four abodes of Brahmā.
Through cultivating giving, moral virtue, patience, vigor,
Meditation, and wisdom, may they thereby be gracefully adorned.

088 / (76)
Becoming perfectly complete in cultivation of merit and wisdom,
Producing the illumination radiating from major and minor marks,
I pray that, through inconceivable and immeasurable conduct,
They will course unhindered through the ten grounds.

089 / (77)
Whatever else might correspond to these meritorious qualities,
May there also be adornment with those other such qualities
As well as liberation from all karmic transgressions.
I pray I shall embody cherishing concern for the welfare of beings.

简体字	正體字
5-090 / (78) 圆满一切善及众生[7]所乐 能除他众苦愿我恒如此	5-090 / (78) 圓滿一切善及眾生[7]所樂 能除他眾苦願我恒如此
5-091 / (79) 若他有怖畏一切时及处 由唯忆我名得脱一切苦	5-091 / (79) 若他有怖畏一切時及處 由唯憶我名得脫一切苦
5-092 / (80) 敬信我及瞋若见及忆持 乃至闻我名愿彼定菩提	5-092 / (80) 敬信我及瞋若見及憶持 乃至聞我名願彼定菩提
5-093 / (81) 愿我得五通恒随一切生 愿我恒能生众生善及乐	5-093 / (81) 願我得五通恒隨一切生 願我恒能生眾生善及樂
5-094 / (82) 若他欲作恶于一切世界 愿遍断彼恶如理令修善	5-094 / (82) 若他欲作惡於一切世界 願遍斷彼惡如理令修善
5-095 / (83) 如地水火风野药及林树 如他欲受用愿我自忍受	5-095 / (83) 如地水火風野藥及林樹 如他欲受用願我自忍受
5-096 / (84ab) 愿我他所爱如念自寿命 愿我念众生[8]万倍胜自爱	5-096 / (84ab) 願我他所愛如念自壽命 願我念眾生[8]萬倍勝自愛
5-097 / (84cd) 愿彼所作恶于我果报熟 是我所行善于彼果报熟	5-097 / (84cd) 願彼所作惡於我果報熟 是我所行善於彼果報熟

Chapter 5: *On Right Practice for Monastics*

090 / (78)
May I completely perfect all forms of goodness
And whatever might conduce to the happiness to beings,
Becoming able to eliminate their manifold sufferings.
I pray I shall always act in this way.

091 / (79)
Should they become afflicted with fear
At any time or place,
Through merely calling to mind my name,
May they straightaway gain liberation from all sufferings.

092 / (80)
Whether extending respectful trust to me or even hating me,
If they but behold me or merely bear me in mind,
Even to the point that they only hear my name,
May they thus be bound for certain success [on the path to] bodhi.[189]

093 / (81)
I pray that I will be able to gain the five superknowledges
And that they will constantly follow me in every succeeding life.[190]
I pray that I will always be able to cause the development
Of goodness in beings while bringing them happiness as well.

094 / (82)
Should they be about to engage in evil deeds
Within any of the worlds,
I pray I will be everywhere able to halt their evil endeavors
And then influence them in a principled way to cultivate goodness.

095 / (83)
Just as they utilize the earth, water, fire, and wind,
The wild herbs, and the forest trees,
So too, in whatever way they wish to put me to use,
I pray I will naturally be able to endure and accept it.

096 / (84ab)
I pray I will be cherished by them
To the same degree that they feel concern for their own lives.
I pray I will maintain a mindful concern for the welfare of beings
Ten thousand times greater than my cherishing of self.

097 / (84cd)
I pray that whatever evil they have done
Will have its fruit of retribution ripen in me
And that this goodness which I practice
Will have its fruit of retribution ripen in them.

简体字	正體字
5-098 / (85) 一人未解脱于有随生道 愿我为彼住不先取菩提	5-098 / (85) 一人未解脫於有隨生道 願我為彼住不先取菩提
5-099 / (86) 能如此修行福德若有体 于恒沙世界其功不可量	5-099 / (86) 能如此修行福德若有體 於恒沙世界其功不可量
5-100 / (87) 佛世尊自说如此因难[9]量 众生界无量利益愿亦尔	5-100 / (87) 佛世尊自說如此因難[9]量 眾生界無量利益願亦爾
5-101 / (88) 此法我略说能生自他利 愿汝爱此法如爱念自身	5-101 / (88) 此法我略說能生自他利 願汝愛此法如愛念自身
5-102 / (89) 若人爱此法是实爱自身 是所爱应憎增此憎增由法成	5-102 / (89) 若人愛此法是實愛自身 是所愛應憎增此憎增由法成
5-103 / (90) 故事法如身事行如事法 如行事慧然如慧事智者	5-103 / (90) 故事法如身事行如事法 如行事慧然如慧事智者
5-104 / (91) 净顺有智慧伏他说正理 由自恶疑他此人损自事	5-104 / (91) 淨順有智慧伏他說正理 由自惡疑他此人損自事

098 / (85)
Should there remain even one person who hasn't gained liberation
And who, abiding in existence, courses on in the paths of rebirth,
I pray I shall continue to abide therein for their benefit,
Refraining from opting for bodhi before they have reached it.

5. THE MERIT OF SUCH CULTIVATION IS INCALCULABLE
099 / (86)
Where one is able to cultivate in this manner,
If the merit generated by it could have a physical substance,
Even a Ganges' sands number of worlds,
Would be inadequate to measure one's merit.

100 / (87)
The Buddha, the Bhagavān, stated himself
That causal bases such as these are immeasurable.
Just as the realms of beings are immeasurable in their vastness,
So, too, are vows dedicated to providing them benefit.

6. CONCLUDING INSTRUCTIONS
101 / (88)
This Dharma which I have only briefly described
Is able to bring about the welfare of both self and others.
I pray your cherishing of this Dharma
Will be as great as your fond concern for your very own person.

102 / (89)
If a person loves this Dharma,
In truth, this is the same as cherishing his own person.
This object of one's affection should be allowed to flourish.
Such flourishing is perfected by resort to Dharma itself.[191]

103 / (90)
Therefore serve the Dharma as attentively as you serve yourself.
Serve the practice as attentively as you serve the Dharma.
As you serve the practice, so too serve wisdom.
And, as you serve wisdom, so too should you serve the wise.

104 / (91)
One should accord in purity with he who is wise
And submit to his instructions on what constitutes right principles.
If, due to one's own evil, one cherishes doubts in such a person,
One would thereby wreak harm upon his very own endeavors.

简体字	正體字
5-105 / (92) 是诸善知识汝应知略相 知足慈悲戒智慧能灭恶	5-105 / (92) 是諸善知識汝應知略相 知足慈悲戒智慧能滅惡
5-106 / (93) 善友应教汝汝知敬顺行 由内外胜德汝必至胜处	5-106 / (93) 善友應教汝汝知敬順行 由內外勝德汝必至勝處
5-107 / (94) 实誓说爱言乐性不可动 正事增谄曲愿汝自易教	5-107 / (94) 實誓說愛言樂性不可動 正事增諂曲願汝自易教
5-108 / (95) 已舍无有悔有焰炽心寂 无懈缓掉动不贡高和同	5-108 / (95) 已捨無有悔有焰熾心寂 無懈緩掉動不貢高和同
5-109 / (96) 愿清凉如月有炽盛如日 甚深如大海坚住如山王	5-109 / (96) 願清涼如月有熾盛如日 甚深如大海堅住如山王
5-110 / (97) 一切果/过所离众德所庄严 众生所受用愿汝一切智	5-110 / (97) 一切果/過所離眾德所莊嚴 眾生所受用願汝一切智
5-111 / (98) 我不但为王说如此善法 如理为馀人由欲利一切	5-111 / (98) 我不但為王說如此善法 如理為餘人由欲利一切
5-112 / (99) 大王此正论汝日日谛听 为令自及他得无上菩提	5-112 / (99) 大王此正論汝日日諦聽 為令自及他得無上菩提

105 / (92)
As for these who serve as good spiritual friends,
You should be aware of their general characteristics.
Easily satisfied, kind, compassionate, and morally restrained,
They are well able, by resorting to wisdom, to eliminate any evil.

106 / (93)
Such a good friend should instruct you
And you should know to respectfully accord with this in practice.
By resort to superior inward and outward qualities,
You may certainly succeed in reaching the most supreme station.[192]

107 / (94)
Be genuine in your vows and kind in your speech.
Be pleasant in nature while also being unshakable.
See that right is done and disdain deviousness.
I pray that you yourself will be easily instructed.

108 / (95)
As for what has been relinquished, have no regrets about it.
Possess a brilliantly energetic spirit attended by a quiescent mind.
Remain free of either indolence or agitation.
Refraining from hypocrisy and engage harmoniously with others.

109 / (96)
I pray you will be clear and cool like the moon,
Will be brimming with brilliance like the sun,
Will be extremely deep like the great seas,
And will be as solidly abiding as the king of mountains,

110 / (97)
May you abandon all faults,[193]
May you become gracefully adorned by the manifold qualities,
And may you serve as a resource for the benefit of beings.
I pray you will gain realization of omniscience.

111 / (98)
It is not solely for the sake of the King
That I have explained here such fine Dharma.
As befits these principles, it is for the rest of the people as well.
This has arisen from my wish to serve the welfare of everyone.

112 / (99)
Great King. As for this treatise on what is right,
You should study it attentively each and every day
For the sake of causing both yourself and others
To realize the unsurpassed bodhi.

5-113 / (100a) 胜戒敬尊长忍辱无嫉妬 不悋财知足救济堕难事 **5-114 / 100b** 能行善恶人摄持及制伏 弘护佛正法求菩提应行 <div align="center">宝行王正论[1]</div>	**5-113 / (100a)** 勝戒敬尊長忍辱無嫉妬 不悋財知足救濟墮難事 **5-114 / 100b** 能行善惡人攝持及制伏 弘護佛正法求菩提應行 <div align="center">寶行王正論[1]</div>
<div align="center">简体字</div>	<div align="center">正體字</div>

113 / (100a)
Be supreme in virtue and reverence to those venerable and senior.
Practice patience and remain free of jealousy.
Refrain from miserliness, realize when enough is enough,
And rescue those who have fallen into difficult circumstances.

114 / (100b)
As for those able to practice goodness and those prone to evil,
Draw in and retain the former. Control and subdue the latter.
As for propagating and protecting the right Dharma of the Buddha
And striving to realize bodhi, one must put these into actual practice.

End of *A Strand of Jewels*
A Discourse Advising the King

Appendix

The Fifty-seven Faults to be Abandoned
(With Sanskrit Antecedents and Chapter 5 *Śloka* Numbers)[194]

1. Anger (*krodha*) - (3)
2. Enmity (*upanāha*) - (3)
3. Concealment (*mrakṣa*) - (3)
4. Deception (*māyā*) - (4)
5. Deviousness (*śāṭhya*) - (4)
6. Jealousy (*īrṣyā*) - (4)
7. Miserliness (*mātsarya*) - (4)
8. Absence of sense of shame (*ahrīkya*) - (5)
9. Absence of dread of blame (*anapatrāpya*) - (5)
10. Non-humility (*asaṃnati*) - (5)
11. Wrathfulness (*saṃrambha*) - (5)
12. [Self]-infatuation (*mada*) - (6)
13. Negligence (*pramāda*) - (6)
14. [Generic] arrogance (*māna*) - (7). There are seven types of "arrogance" of which this is the first.
15. Elevating arrogance (*atimāna*) - (8)
16. Over-reaching arrogance (*māna-atimāna*) - (9)
17. Self-imputing arrogance (*asmi-māna*) - (10)
18. Overweening arrogance (*abhi-māna*) - (11)
19. Perverse arrogance (*mithyā-māna*) - (11)
20. Arrogance in inferiority (*adhamo māna*). This may be further divided into two subtypes, both of which are found in the Chinese edition of this text: The "outwardly-directed" subtype is found in what appears to be an interpolated commentarial extra verse located between *śloka* 7 and *śloka* 8. The "inwardly-directed" subtype, found in all editions of the text, is contained in *śloka* 12. It seems fairly clear that this "arrogance in inferiority" is meant to occur only once in Nāgārjuna's list of 57 faults and so it is that I count it only once herein.
21. Hypocrisy (*kuhanā*) - (13)
22. Flattery (*lapanā*) - (13)
23. Hinting (*naimittikatva*) - (14)
24. Coercion through reproval (*naiṣpeṣikatvam*) - (14)

25. Seeking gains from gains (*lābhena lipsā lābhānā*) - (15)
26. Quiet condemnation (*?)- (15)
27. Immobilizing anxiety (*staimitya*) - (16)
28. Multifarious thinking (*nānātva-saṃjñā*) - (17)
29. Non-reflectiveness (*amanaskāra*) - (17)
30. Disrespectfulness (*?)- (18)
31. Irreverence (*?)- (18)
32. Attachment (*gardha*) - (19)
33. Pervasive attachment (*pari-gardha*) - (19)
34. Avarice (*lobha*) - (20)
35. Inordinate avarice (*viṣamo lobha*) - (20)
36. Evil lust (*pāpecchatā*) - (21)
37. Extreme desire (*mahecchatā*) - (22)
38. Desire for recognition (*icchepsutā*) - (22)
39. Non-forbearance (*akṣānti*) - (23)
40. Impropriety (*anācāra*) - (23)
41. Refractoriness to instruction (*daurvacasya*) - (24)
42. Kinship ideation (*jñāti-sambandho-vitarka*) - (24)
43. Region-related ideation (*jānapada-vitarka*) - (25)
44. Immortality ideation (*amara-vitarka*) - (25)
45. Recognition-dependent ideation (*anu-vijñapti-saṃyukto-vitarka*) - (26)
46. Harmful ideation (*Conjectural: *vihiṃsā-vitarka*) - (27)
47. Uneasiness (*arati*) - (28)
48. Exhaustion (*tandrā*) - (28)
49. Indolence (*ālasya*) - (28)
50. Distorted physical expression (*vijṛmbhikā*) - (29)
51. Food intoxication (*bhakta-sammada*) - (29)
52. Mental depression (*ceto-līnatvam*) - (30)

Nāgārjuna's list concludes with "the five hindrances" consisting of seven components. By a convention traceable to the origins of Buddhism, four of those seven components (*styāna-middha* and *auddhatya-kaukṛtya*) compose "double-component hindrances." Hence, for the purposes of Nāgārjuna's list, these seven components are construed as being only five in number.

53. Desire (*kāma-chanda*) - (30)
54. Ill-will (*vyāpāda*) - (31)
55. a) Lethargy; b) Drowsiness (*styāna-middha*) - (32)
56. a) Excitedness; b) Regretfulness (*auddhatya-kaukṛtya*) - (33)
57. Doubtfulness (*vicikitsā*) - (33)

Endnotes

1. For an extensive discussion of the life of Nāgārjuna, see the second chapter ("Early Indian Mādhyamika") of Richard Robinson's *Early Mādhyamika in India and China*. For an extended summary of the various Tibetan scriptural bases for assigning Nāgārjuna a lifespan of many hundreds of years, see the first chapter ("Nāgārjuna's Biography from Tibetan Sources") of Jeffrey Hopkins' *Buddhist Advice for Living and Liberation*).
2. The digital edition chosen as the basis of this translation is from CBETA 2004 which in turn corresponds to Taisho 1656. Taisho records 100-odd variants from alternate editions of the Chinese text. Most of those are clearly just scribal errors. Where I find evidence for adopting an emendation, it is signaled in these notes.
3. This according to Michael Hahn in *Nāgārjuna's Ratnāvalī*, 1982, p. 14.
4. "Adorned with the perfected qualities" likely refers to repletion in the two provisions essential for highest bodhi (*bodhisaṃbhāra*, specifically merit and wisdom), "adornment" with which is emblematically manifest in the 32 major physical marks and 80 minor physical characteristics unique to the body of a buddha.
5. "Omniscient Honored One" is a reference to the Buddha.
6. "True good friend of beings" in the Chinese corresponds to the "sole friend of all beings" in the Sanskrit (*sarvasattvaikabāndhavam*).
7. "Vessel of Dharma" is a standard image in Buddhism referring to whomsoever has developed the capacity to correctly comprehend the Dharma, realize the fruits of its Path, and then pass the Dharma on to ensuing generations.
8. Faith and wisdom are the first two members in a Buddhist standard list of "five root-faculties" which consist of faith, vigor, mindfulness, concentration, and wisdom. When fully developed these become known as the "five powers."

    Regarding "Due to faith, one becomes able to uphold the Dharma": The most striking feature of this passage is that it states so clearly what an indispensable role faith plays in one's ability to take up the practices essential to realizing the Path. Although, as stated, "of the two, wisdom is superior," genuine wisdom will still never arise in the absence of faith and the path practices flowing forth from it. Hence, without faith, one will never succeed in "gaining comprehension corresponding to reality" and thus one will never succeed in gaining liberation, period.

Nāgārjuna speaks extensively on the crucial role of faith as the primary essential through which one becomes able to enter the Dharma of the buddha, most notable early on in his commentary on the *Great Perfection of Wisdom Sutra*.

9. Nāgārjuna here makes a startling assertion, the truth of which is finally undeniable. He claims in essence that perfecting such a seemingly simple skill as consistent restraint in physical, verbal, and mental karma is actually what serves as the basis of genuine wisdom. The implications of this are ironic and even humorous: The mere ability to carefully monitor and artfully restrain one's own body, mouth, and mind can make one equal or even superior in one's wisdom to all of those pandits who exhaust their entire lives in the industrious pursuit of refined knowledge and wisdom.

By way of defining the specific meaning of ethical restraints on body, mouth, and mind, Nāgārjuna introduces in the following two *ślokas* the ten unwholesome karmic deeds, a standard and often-encountered formulation common to all schools of Buddhism. They originate from the Buddha himself. Whereas the five precepts are commonly referred to as the causes whereby one secures continued rebirth in the human realm, the ten good karmic deeds are commonly cited as the causes by which one may ensure rebirth in the heavens.

10. Although refraining from consumption of intoxicants and pure livelihood are contained in principle in the ten good karmic deeds with the former implicit in abstaining from wrong views and the latter implicit in the abstention from harming associated with not killing, not stealing, not committing sexual misconduct, and not lying, still, they are not listed in so many words. Hence Nāgārjuna makes a point of specifically listing them here.

11. I suggest here the bracketed emendation involving the addition of "and patience" because it is present in both the surviving Sanskrit and Tibetan, because its replacement in this line by the word "cultivation" is almost certainly a scribal error (hence *xiu* [修] should be *ren* [忍]), and because Nāgārjuna elsewhere points to these first three perfections as constituting the collective bases for generating the "provision" of merit (this in his commentary on the *Great Perfection of Wisdom Sutra*). In addition to being one of the two "provisions" (*saṃbhāra*) essential to buddhahood, merit is the primary cause of happiness, the very topic of the current discussion.

Nāgārjuna does not reference the final three perfections (vigor, meditative discipline, and wisdom) in this *śloka* because those are the causes leading to the development of the "provision" of wisdom which is more fundamentally a cause of "liberation," the topic which will follow immediately upon this discussion of happiness.

12. As for the reference to the ascetic practice of voluntarily taking on a life emulating that of particular species of animals, this sort of non-beneficial asceticism was not uncommon among early Indian non-Buddhist religious sects. Because such practices were rooted in ignorance and bound not to bring about any spiritually liberating result, they were often criticized in Buddhist commentarial literature.

13. Having already referred in the previous three *ślokas* to the pointlessness of non-beneficial forms of asceticism, Nāgārjuna now describes, specifically in reference to the form of asceticism which involves emulating the simple life of a cow, what the likely outcome of such asceticism would be when examined according to basic and obvious causality principles. Such asceticism does not in fact lead to some sort of spiritual awakening attendant upon such voluntary simplicity, but rather leads in the longer term to just those very sorts of life circumstances to which cows themselves fall prey, namely hunger, thirst, oppressive heat from the baking sun, and repeated deaths as a victim to beasts of prey, this across the course of many such lifetimes.

One might well ask why Nāgārjuna devotes this much space to discrediting non-beneficial forms of asceticism. It is not unlikely that such an approach to spiritual practice was widely admired at the time. It may even have been the case that such practices occupied the uncritical thought and discourse of the king or kings to whom this work is nominally addressed. Thus this would just be an instance of addressing the Dharma teachings to the specific conditions prevailing in the intended audience for Nāgārjuna's work.

14. The topic of this passage is typical karmic retributions corresponding to the three negative physical karmas from among the ten unwholesome karmic deeds, namely killing, stealing, and sexual misconduct. It is because physically tormenting others is a common karmic error closely related to the transgression of killing that Nāgārjuna also brings up that specific topic along with one of its primary negative karmic retributions. The final line's "invading another's domain" is a euphemistic reference to the sexual misconduct transgression which here specifically points to an adulterous liaison or to instances of sexually preying on unemancipated persons "under the protection" of their families.

Were it not for the constraints of space, Nāgārjuna might well have pointed out other negative karmic retributions for these four offenses. For instance, orthodox Buddhist instruction on causality teaches that killing may lead not only to an early death, but also to a death which is particularly painful, violent, and degrading. It teaches that physically tormenting others may lead not only to sickness, but also to being subjected to torment and abuse oneself. It teaches that stealing may result not just in poverty, but also in being constantly stolen from and in constantly being mistrusted. It also teaches that sexual misconduct results not just in a multitude of adversaries but also in having one's own subsequent-lifetime intimates inclined toward interpersonal dishonesty and sexual involvements with persons outside of the primary relationship.

15. "Frivolous speech" as a Buddhist technical term refers not solely to wasting time by talking about irrelevant and distracting topics. Rather it refers as well to lewd speech, crude speech, and off-color jokes as well. Perhaps the most conservative and useful interpretation of "frivolous speech" might define it as any discourse which does not directly conduce to advancement on the Path. The four topics of this śloka are the four negative karmic deeds associated with the mouth which, together with the three associated with the physical actions, and the three associated with the mind, make up the ten unwholesome karmic deeds.

16. In these next six ślokas, Nāgārjuna concludes his discussion of the part of this first chapter which is devoted most directly to explaining the causes for happiness, after which he proceeds in the twenty-fifth śloka to take up his treatment of the causes of liberation.

    In this particular passage, Nāgārjuna sums up his treatment of the ten unwholesome karmic deeds and the associated negative karmic practices by indicating that those are the bases for undergoing all of the painful karmic retributions just outlined above, noting also that it is the ten good karmic deeds and their associated positive karmic practices which constitute the bases of good karma bound to produce desirable karmic consequences.

17. Śloka 19c-d and śloka 20a-b, missing from the Chinese, have been restored from the Sanskrit. They were probably accidentally dropped at some point along the line either due to scribal error or due to misperceiving the two lines of text as accidentally introduced redundancies in need of excision.

18. The two-character phrase 惡修 (more commonly 惡趣 or 惡道) is a somewhat non-standard early Sino-Buddhist translation of the Sanskrit *durgati*, "wretched destiny," a reference to the realms of the animals, ghosts, and hells.

19. The referent of "these two dharmas" should be obvious: 1) the avoidance of evil, and 2) the practice of goodness. I point this out only because there does exist a single Tibetan edition (*zhol*) which speaks of "three" instead of "two" in this śloka, explained by Gyel-tsap

(as reported by Hopkins) as referencing the karmic actions of body, mouth, and mind. This is clearly not Nāgārjuna's intent, however, for two of the Tibetan editions, the Ajitamitra commentary, the Sanskrit, and this very early Chinese edition all speak of "two," not "three."

20. "Four [unfortunate] destinies" refers to the realms of the *asuras*, animals, hungry ghosts, and hells. The Sanskrit and Tibetan editions apparently reference only the standard three "wretched destinies" (*durgati*), thus leaving aside as implicit the unfortunate circumstance of an *asura* rebirth.

    A note on *asuras*: Asuras exist as a completely separate "demigod" or "titan" rebirth category among "the six destinies." They are characterized by a fondness for contentiousness and struggle, the previous-life karmic causes for which include hatefulness, jealousy, and merit markedly inferior to that of even the lowest levels of gods. They are often portrayed as locked in a sort of perpetual celestial *jihad* with the lower-level gods inhabiting the more subtle strata of the desire realm.

21. "Concentrations" refers specifically to the four *dhyānas*. "Brahmavihāras" is another name for the four "immeasurable minds" (*apramāṇa-citta*). These consist of kindness, compassion, sympathetic joy, and even-mindedness.

    "Formless absorptions" renders Paramārtha's one character abbreviation: "space" (空), here a condensation of a more common 3-character Chinese rendering of "the four formless absorptions" (四空處). This refers specifically to the four formless-realm stations: "infinite space," "infinite consciousness," "nothing whatsoever," and "neither perception nor non-perception."

22. "The bliss of Brahmā and the others" is a general reference to the exquisite and long-enduring bliss enjoyed by the form-realm and formless-realm gods whilst residing in their various celestial abodes.

23. The *skandhas* or "aggregates" (form, feeling, perception, karmic formative factors, and consciousness) serve as the very basis upon which one generates the false notion of a "self" in the first place. Then, however, the attachment to this false notion of a "self" in turn precipitates further instances of generation of the aggregates themselves, this through the mechanism of the twelve-fold causal chain. Thus a fundamental delusion about the nature of reality produces an endlessly-repeated cycle of events involving feeling, craving, grasping and so forth until we come to birth, aging, and death. When repeated, this produces rebirth after rebirth.

24. "Meaning" here translates *yi* (義). It could as easily be rendered as "reason" (which would point to the rational progressions of analytic

contemplation culminating in realization of a self's "emptiness" of inherent existence). Here, however, it is perhaps more properly understood in terms of its other primary sense in these contexts: "highest truth" (第一義諦), the Sino-Buddhist rendering of the Sanskrit *paramārtha-satya*.

25. "Seed" here is a metaphor for "self." "Sprout" is a metaphor for the five aggregates and also for the false concept of anything belonging to a self.

26. The first two feet of this *śloka* reiterate the interdependent linkage of attachment to the aggregates and the habitual and continual generation of the view clinging to the idea of an inherently existent "self."

    Nāgārjuna next sets forth the true import of this fact: The twelve-fold chain of causation shall remain unbroken so long as we retain attachment to the view clinging to existence of a self. Based on ignorance-based delusion, we shall continue to initiate "karmic actions" (the second of the causal links) and all of the other links in the causal chain, the result being that we shall continue to generate "becoming" (the tenth link), thus precipitating subsequent rebirths. Consequently our own personal wheel of uncontrolled suffering in cyclic existence shall continue to cycle on endlessly until we gain deep realizations on the Path.

27. "The three component phases" of the twelve-fold chain of causes and conditions are as follows:

    The first two (ignorance and karmic action) correlate most directly to the past.

    The next eight (consciousness, name-and-form; the six sense faculties, contact, feeling, craving, grasping, becoming) correlate most directly with the present.

    The last two (birth and aging-and-death) correlate most directly with the future.

    Nāgārjuna notes that, in spite of these "stock" correlations, in fact, none of these three component phases "may be deemed to be 'prior,' 'intermediary,' or 'subsequent'." This is because, depending on the manner in which one analyzes the twelve-fold chain, each of the twelve component "links" may be said to belong to any of the three periods of time.

    The twelve-fold chain of causes and conditions, what Nāgārjuna refers to here as "the wheel of cyclic births and deaths," serves as the mechanism by which one rolls on endlessly through births and deaths on the "wheel" of cyclic existence. It is because this twelve-fold chain remains unbroken that beings needlessly subject themselves to uncontrolled alternations between long tours of extreme sufferings and relatively infrequent enjoyments of celestial blisses. The "unbroken" nature of this cycle is the subject of Nāgārjuna's analogy wherein he compares it to the appearance of a continuous "wheel" manifest by "the twirling of a firebrand."

The actual workings of the twelve-fold chain of causes and conditions are not immediately obvious. The Buddha indicated as much and most who have tried to understand it would agree. In fact, complete fathoming of its mechanisms would itself finally precipitate liberation from cyclic existence. (After all, this is how a "pratyekabuddha" becomes enlightened and becomes able to abandon cyclic existence.) A reasonably complete discussion may be found in Chapter Three of Vasubandhu's *Treatise on the Treasury of Dharmic Analysis* (*Abhidharma-kośa-bhāṣyam*).

28. For the proofs regarding non-production from self, from other, or from both, and for the proof of the unreality of existence in any of the three periods of time, see Nāgārjuna's *Treatise on the Middle*. Nāgārjuna informs us here that once we gain realization of the truth of the claims made in the first two feet of this *śloka*, attachment to the existence of an inherently existent self will be brought to a halt.

The consequence of that would be that karmic actions rooted in clinging to a self would also be brought to a halt. Finally, there would then no longer be any possibility of having to undergo additional negative karmic retributions arising from unenlightened actions, principally because no more unenlightened causal actions could be initiated.

It is not the case that there are no longer any karmic actions performed in the *ārya's* karmic continuum. It is just that those karmic actions are free of error and thus are not generative of negative karmic retributions. Also, karmic retribution does indeed continue to be operative. In the case of the *ārya*, he no longer initiates karma which would produce a negative retribution and, when faced with undergoing negative karmic retributions from previously generated negative karmic actions, because he is liberated from attachment to a "self," he is also liberated from seizing upon negative karmic retributions as involving "suffering."

29. Nāgārjuna clarifies here the nature of the ontological "stance" of one who has gained realization of right view with respect to how worldly phenomena exist, how they are created, how they are destroyed, and how they are neither produced nor destroyed. He informs us that a being who has gained this realization no longer seizes upon worldly conventional existence as genuinely reflecting ultimate reality. Additionally, even though such a being is entirely cognizant that all worldly phenomena and all beings possess no valid inherent or permanent existence, still, he does not seize upon "non-existence" as

a stance reflecting ultimate reality, either.

30. It should not be surprising that the untutored worldling tends to be shaken by a sort of fearfulness when informed by the Āryas that the "self" and the "world" are not ultimately real. This "fear" is perhaps an analogue of the fear of being robbed and murdered, for it is almost as if "emptiness" threatens confiscation of the "self" along with all of its supposed possessions.

   Nāgārjuna points out that, given that this teaching brings the end of all suffering, fearfulness is baseless and unreasonable. When he speaks of "that station in which one has nothing to fear," he is referring to nirvāṇa.

31. This śloka and the next are addressed primarily to those who seek the nirvāṇa realized through the path of arhatship. They already accept that neither self nor aggregates exist in nirvāṇa. Still, they tend to find difficulty in accepting the emptiness teachings through which one may realize nirvāṇa even while abiding in the world. Nāgārjuna in effect asks them, "Since you don't fear the prospect of cessation when presented as that nirvāṇa which is the culmination of your arhat path, why do you now fear this teaching explaining all phenomena as devoid of any intrinsically real existence?"

32. I emend here the *Taisho* version of the text (substituting *ling* [令] for *jin* [今]), this in order to correct an obvious scribal error. This graphically-similar variant is found in three other editions. Additional evidence for adopting the variant is the intentional parallelism with the structure of the ensuing *śloka*.

   As Nāgārjuna implies in the text, failure to align one's thoughts, words, and deeds to the ever-potent dictates of cause-and-effect will eliminate any possibility of amassing the immense amount of merit required for buddhahood. Beyond that, such a karmic stance will also result in the rapid destruction of any merit already created in past and present lives.

33. As Nāgārjuna states in his *Treatise on the Provisions Essential for Enlightenment* (*Bodhisaṃbhāra Śāstra*), "a full measure of merit" refers to an amount of merit so massive as to rival the size of Mount Sumeru. It requires just such an extensive amount of merit linked to just such a massive amount of wisdom to be able to succeed in gaining buddhahood.

   "Good destinies" here is intended to refer to the precise opposite of the "wretched destinies" referred to in the previous *śloka*. In concrete terms, this is a reference to rebirth among humans and gods.

34. "Tantamount to gaining liberation" simply means that, by abiding in wisdom constantly cognizant of "wrong view" and "right view" (as defined in the previous two *ślokas*), one's practice will remain correct

and will eventually lead to liberation. Additionally, one will also gain liberation even now from struggling with dual concepts obsessing on "existence" versus "non-existence," and so forth. Of course cause-and-effect as the ever-present basis of karmic law will certainly always remain in force, but because one's causal actions guided by wisdom naturally accord with it, then the quality of future effects is already assured.

35. This *śloka* is anchored in what we term "conventional" or "relative" truth. Although at the level of ultimate truth, "causation" can be refuted as an ultimately-existent process, at the level of conventional truth, interdependent causation is entirely obvious and defensible. Given the tendency of Buddhist dialectics to point out that "emptiness" of inherent existence is the basic state of affairs for all phenomena, it would be easy for the incautious Dharma student to fall into a view clinging to the idea that all phenomena are "non-existent."

    Nāgārjuna counters this potential problem by pointing out that one need only examine the causal bases for the conventional existence of any phenomenon and then note that the arising of any phenomenon is the product of the temporary conjunction of multiple causes and conditions. One is forced to admit then that, on the level of relative truth, there is indeed a temporary conventional existence to phenomena. This serves to effectively antidote the tendency to fall into a nihilistic view asserting conventionally-existent phenomena to be utterly "non-existent."

    The next line points out that, in order to abandon attachment to asserting any phenomenon's supposed real existence, one need only look more closely at the process of destruction of any such phenomenon. One quickly recognizes that any given phenomenon's existence could only have been recognized as valid in the first place on the basis of a merely temporary conjunction of impermanent causes and conditions. Once even one of these causes or conditions deteriorates, then the given phenomenon's destruction ensues. Hence "existence" collapses as well. When contemplating this, one will successfully antidote any tendency to fall into asserting phenomena as genuinely "existent."

36. Nāgārjuna refutes these theories of causation in his *Shāstra on the Middle*. He also discusses and explains there the concepts brought up in the next few *ślokas*.

37. This and the previous *śloka* illustrate the unreality of concepts which are polar or otherwise interdependent. "Long" as a designation has no meaning in the absence "short." So, too, in the case of a "lantern" which gains meaning as a designation only in dependence on its ability to generate illumination. Take for example the case of a candle

lantern. Unless there is actually a flame burning inside of it, referring to it as a "lantern" is really only a provisional sort of designation not actually reflecting any presently real circumstance.

38. Although, in terms of ultimate truth, phenomena have no objective inherent existence of their own, still, at the level of conventional or relative truth: 1) There actually is a process of serial production of phenomena; 2) There actually is a coincidence of events whereby temporary causes and conditions come together to produce any given phenomenon; and 3) There actually is a meaningful basis for applying interdependent and polarity-based designations to merely conventionally-existent phenomena. Given this merely provisional level of reality, one has to admit that, at least on the level of relative truth, it would be absurd to claim that such phenomena have no valid conventional existence. This is the point of the first two feet of this *śloka*.

Still, in the absence of this sort of analytic understanding of the nature of conventional existence, one may maintain in the manner of the foolish common person the unquestioning assumption that things exist as real entities in and of themselves. Nāgārjuna makes it clear here that this sort of unquestioning assumption is the product of a mind which makes erroneous imputations based on delusion. This is the point of the final two feet of this *śloka*.

39. Adopting here the variant found in four other editions apparently originating in a scribal error involving graphically-similar characters, this by substituting 色 for Taisho's 已. In truth, even the apparently erroneous version may be construed with equally good sense.

40. In these next five *ślokas*, Nāgārjuna uses one of a standard set of ten "emptiness" similes to illustrate the absence of inherent existence in the world, the self, the aggregates, and all dharmas. The other nine similes (which he discusses at length in his commentary on the *Great Perfection of Wisdom Sutra*) are: like a magically-conjured illusion, like the moon reflected in water, like empty space, like an echo, like the city of the gandharvas, like a dream, like a shadow, like an image in a mirror, and like a supernatural transformation. The meaning of the analogy in the five *ślokas* is so profoundly presented in the context of Nāgārjuna's ongoing argument that, when meditated upon, it may serve as the cause for a profound awakening.

41. The import of the first two feet of the *śloka*: When one "seizes on non-existence," i.e. "annihilationism," this typically entails a denial that death is anything other than a complete departure from any sort of existence. Hence there is a tendency then to discount the reality of multiple lifetimes, cause-and-effect, and karmic retribution for present-life physical, verbal, and mental actions. The result: one may engender disastrous karmic consequences, the worst-case scenario

being rebirth in the "three wretched destinies" (*durgati*) corresponding to the realms of the animals, *pretas* ("hungry ghosts," etc.), and hells.

The import of the second two feet of the *śloka*: This refers to the opposite wrong view known as "eternalism." When one believes strongly in the true "existence" of the world and the beings in it, one is far more prone to take seriously teachings on multiple lifetimes, cause-and-effect, and karmic retribution for present-life actions. The result: One is more likely to avoid negative actions, engage in good ones, and produce a bright and fortunate future karmic scenario. Unfortunately, this conviction tends to be overcome by the force of delusion-generated afflictions and unskillful karma in later lives. That in turn precipitates another fall, and so the endless transit between the heavens and the hells continues on unabated, even in this seemingly "positive" case referenced in the second foot of the *śloka*.

The import of the last half of the *śloka*: When one finally fathoms the nature of ultimate reality, one is able to dispense with attachment to either pole of the "non-existence versus existence" duality. The result: One becomes free of all attachments, understands all things, and gains the liberation which, through ongoing direct perception of the emptiness of all phenomena, naturally compels one to refrain from karmic error. Hence one becomes freed from endless uncontrolled coursing in cyclic existence involving brief sojourns to the heavens followed by long tours of duty in the lower realms.

42. This *śloka* and the next two constitute Nāgārjuna's response to the charge that refusing to validate views asserting ultimacy of either "existence" or "non-existence" somehow reflects an implicit fall into a nihilistic attachment as one's default metaphysical stance. Nāgārjuna points out here that such nihilism indictments are absurd.

    Why does Nāgārjuna hold that such nihilism indictments are absurd? It is because of the inherent duality involved in "non-existence-attachment" versus "existence-attachment." Hence any such supposed "fall" should be equally likely to "land" in either pole of the duality-based concept. Consequently "disapproval" of subscribing to either attachment might just as easily involve instead a fall into realism, i.e. into that stance which validates the ultimate reality of "existence." Conclusion: The charge that "Not being fond of attachments to either 'existence' or 'non-existence'" is somehow nihilistic therefore falls on its face as an inherently absurd assertion.

43. This *śloka* is essentially a reiteration of Nāgārjuna's refutation of the charge of "implicit nihilism" leveled against his validating disapproval of both existence and non-existence attachments. He once again turns the challenger's argument back on itself, this by using

the force of its absurd implications.

44. Nāgārjuna once again refutes the challenger's claim that Buddhists fall into implicit nihilism (referred to here as "validating non-existence"), doing so by pointing again to the absurd and opposite implications of any such accusation (namely, that it would be just as reasonable to assert this entails falling into realism, here referred to as "validating existence"). But Nāgārjuna goes an extra step here in the first half of this śloka, laying forth a statement describing the basis for refraining from approving the ultimacy of either nihilist or realist positions:

   Nāgārjuna explains that, on account of reliance on bodhi, the transcendent perspective involving awakening to the nature of ultimate reality, Buddhists therefore do not assert any ultimate reality in any particular verbal formulations, any particular physical actions, or any particular configurations of thought, this because any such assertions would entail falling into erroneous views not genuinely reflective of ultimate reality.

45. Nāgārjuna points out in this śloka that Buddhist doctrine is unique in escaping entrapment in the "non-existence versus existence" duality. This could be a point targeted specifically at the King who may well have been "lobbied" by proponents of the non-Buddhist schools mentioned in the śloka. Beyond this, the śloka is directing its assertion of the uniquely transcendent nature of Buddhist doctrine to all who would read this treatise-like "Advice for the King" in the future.

46. Nāgārjuna discusses the unreality of the three periods of time in Chapters Two and Nineteen of his *Treatise on the Middle*.

47. The last two feet of śloka 64 and the first two feet of śloka 65, lost in the Chinese, have been restored here from the extant Sanskrit.

48. Nāgārjuna discusses the unreality of the three marks of production, abiding, and destruction in Chapter Seven of his *Treatise on the Middle*.

49. A kṣaṇa equals one nineteenth of a finger-snap, this by a common traditional definition. The Chinese text sometimes transliterates the term as *chana* (剎那), in which case I reconstruct the Sanskrit. More commonly, it uses another common Chinese rendering for the term, namely *nian* (念), which I render as "instant."

50. The point here: Since we can't even validly establish the inherent "existence" of any dharma in the first place, what's the point in talking about the means by which it might be rendered "non-existent"?

51. As shall be noted, the Buddha's silence was not an issue of being somehow "stumped" by the question, but was rather one of the question itself being based on the false premise of the supposed "existence" of dharmas which cannot be established as possessing any inherent

valid existence. Of course there is the additional factor of the questioner himself being utterly incapable of understanding a response rooted in highest truth. So too with the other thirteen among the fourteen questions upon which the Buddha offered only silence in response.

52. "Those with no capacity to comprehend it" is my less-than-literal rendering of the semi-technical concept: "Those who are not 'receptacles' [fit for retaining the Dharma]."

53. Through a "forced" approach to translating the last half of this *śloka*, one might consider rendering it thus: "Through reliance on this, one remains free of inverted views regarding 'unity' versus 'separation' and 'existence' versus 'non-existence,' those two types of attachments." Because this would involve allowing a syntax violation, an unexpected turn in the argument, and a barely justifiable elevation of the "unity-versus-separation" duality to a prominence equal with the "existence-versus-non-existence" duality, I'm passing on that translation option. The effect on the argument flow would be nil in any case.

54. "Merit" versus "non-merit," though interdependent duality-based concepts, are certainly valid and essential concerns bearing strongly on a host of crucial issues associated with the Path. Still, they do not, in and of themselves, bear such a strong correlation with the wisdom upon which liberation is based. The most profound teachings focus much more strongly on the destruction of delusion through the development of transcendent wisdom. Hence the issue of merit versus non-merit is set aside when focusing on explanation of higher tenets.

55. The point in refraining from laying out the most profound teachings for beings attached to superficial appearances is that they will be unable to accept them without extensive prior preparation. Consequently they are prone to slander higher tenets and the teachers who set them forth, thus generating seriously negative karmic obstacles for themselves. Given that this is such an important issue for the bodhisattva, Nāgārjuna devotes considerable space to laying forth skillful stratagems for teaching people with such widely varying levels of understanding later on in this treatise.

56. Nāgārjuna discusses the six elements at length in Chapter Five of his *Treatise on the Middle*.

57. Nāgārjuna discusses the "fire and fuel" analogy in Chapter Ten of his *Treatise on the Middle*.

58. "Manifestation of predominance" refers to the common circumstance wherein a single "elemental phase" is so dominant that its presence obscures the potential manifestation of the other three. Take for

instance many naturally occurring compounds where, when frozen, the solidity of the "earth element" dominates, when melted, the cohesion of the "water element" dominates, when brought to a vaporizing boil, the "wind element" may manifest dominance in a "blast" of hot gas, and when ignited, combustion manifests dominance of the "fire element."

59. Although not listed in so many words, here as in Nāgārjuna's other writings, a listing of the primary components of a common standard list such as the "eighteen sense realms" or "twelve-fold causal chain" is usually a cue to the reader to infer that the rest of the list is implicitly intended.

60. The references in these *ślokas* to the "demolition," "destruction," "burning up," and "bringing to an utter end" of all worldly phenomena refer to the ability of wisdom to see through to the complete absence of inherent existence of such phenomena. There is no intent to claim that such phenomena have no conventionally valid existence on the level of conventional truth. Rather these statements are all made with reference to the reality revealed at the level of ultimate truth.

61. Again, the mentioning of the first members of a list usually infers the intention to include the remaining members of the list as well, hence my translation's bracketed *"et cetera."* Nāgārjuna's intention here is to refer to sense experience at any of the six sense gates (eye, ear, nose, tongue, body, intellectual mind faculty), hence, when "spelled out," it would read: "As for statements based on knowing via seeing, hearing, smelling, tasting, touching, or intellectually perceiving...".

62. This is a reference to four of various questions deliberately "set aside" and not answered by the Buddha. Standard enumerations vary between ten and fourteen and, in the lists of fourteen, the entities about which they are asked vary somewhat, though the underlying questions remain largely the same. Various reasons are offered in the literature for the Buddha's declining to answer. Some obvious problems with the questions are as follows:

1) The questions themselves are all entirely framed in the language of delusion, thus requiring an answer equally framed in delusion. (This is the very issue referenced by the first line of Nāgārjuna's *śloka*: "Where all dharmas at issue universally fail to accord [with reality]...")

For the purpose of illustration, here are a few *reductio ad absurdum* examples of this sort of question: "What color is turtle fur?"; "What does the child of a eunuch and a barren woman look like?"; "How do you make ghee from milk obtained by tugging on a bull's horn?"

2) Only *āryas* (those who cognize emptiness directly) could genuinely understand the ultimate truth of these matters in any case;

3) Obsession with such questions leads away from liberation, not toward it.

4) The nature of any attempt at an answer would necessarily vary, depending on whether the frame of reference was ultimate truth or conventional truth. This fact alone would make a "definitive" answer impossible.

The ensuing discussion makes it clear that other issues from among the fourteen are inferred. Hence the translation includes the bracketed phrase: *"et cetera."*

That list of fourteen questions finds variant iterations in the canonical literature regarding whether the entity at issue is "the world" or "the world and the self" (in 1-8), whether the entity at issue is "The Tathāgata" or "the soul" (in 9-12), and whether the entities at issue are "the vital principle and the body" or "the soul and the body" (in 13-14). Another common version makes 5-8 a question dealing with the boundedness or unboundedness of the number of beings. That is one of the topics directly addressed in this passage. The fourteen are as follows:

1-8) The questions regarding whether the world (or "the world and the self") is eternal, or not, or both, or neither, bounded, unbounded, both, or neither (In some versions, 5-8 are asked regarding the number of beings);

9-12) The questions regarding whether the Tathāgata (or "the soul") exists after death, or not, or both, or neither;

13-14) The questions regarding whether the "vital principle" (or "the soul") is identical with the body or different from the body.

Again, the Buddha made it clear that when the unenlightened become obsessed with such inexpressible profundities, it leads them not toward liberation, but rather into a web of frivolous dialectical theorizations and disputations constituting a hindrance to liberation.

63. The challenge refers here to the salvific power of the Buddhas figuring in the diminishing of the number of beings across the course of the three periods of time. This is based on the Buddhas' cumulatively causing so many beings to become liberated from cyclic existence. The implication is that, indeed, this was precisely the intention of the Buddha, hence that very fact shows a contradiction in the Buddha's declining to make any definitive assertion on the boundedness, boundlessness, both, or neither of the number of beings in the cosmos.

64. Adopting the variant (of 象 for 像) found in three other editions.

65. Same emendation as above.

66. This *śloka*, lost from the Chinese, is here restored and translated from Tucci's edit of a very late Nepalese Sanskrit edition.

67. I'm correcting a scribal error by emending the text here with a variant reading (離 instead of 誰) found in three other editions.
68. "Compelled to speak in terms of the tetralemma" refers to being forced by the framing of a question to answer it in its own tetralemma-based terms, that is to say in terms of four "choices" between: 1) affirmation; 2) negation; 3) both affirmation and negation; or 4) neither affirmation nor negation.
69. The point here is that the tetralemma-based questions presented to the Buddha were all framed in inherently false terms (not unlike the classic question about the qualities of the son of a eunuch and a barren woman). The Buddha's declining to make definitive statements on such matters on the implicit grounds that such questions present only inherently false choices was entirely justifiable and hence entirely free of fault.
70. "Three types of karmic actions" refers to those created through body, mouth, and mind.
71. "And the rest" is meant to refer at minimum to the rest of the six perfections, namely: vigor, meditative discipline, and wisdom.
72. This is an explicit recitation of the bodhisattva's four means of attraction (*catuḥ-saṃgraha-vastu*). Although the first three, "giving" (*dāna*), "pleasing words" (*priyavacana*), and "beneficial actions" (*arthakṛtya*), are reasonably straightforward, the fourth, translated here as "salutary joint endeavors" (*samānārthatā*), may seem opaque without further explanation: The reference here is to one of the strategies used by the bodhisattva to address circumstances where a person is not otherwise amenable to direct teaching of even the most elementary principles of karmic goodness. In such a case, it may be necessary to first develop with such persons the trust which grows uniquely between friends as they pursue mutual interests together.
73. Those mystified by my rendering of the second foot of this *śloka* may be assisted by contemplating the little-used original definition of the Chinese character *mi* (靡): "the banks of a stream." That this is the intended definition here is cued by the character's juxtaposition with the preceding character, *liu* (流), "to flow" which in turn references "the flowing forth (i.e. 'downstream effect') of sincere intentions."

    Hence, phrased another way, the meaning is: "The power of the flowing forth of good intentions to eliminate opposition is inherently constrained ('banked') by the practical consideration of whether or not those good intentions will actually result in beneficial effects." Obviously, if good intentions are not skillfully directed, they might just as easily produce massive opposition, revolt, and loss of the throne.

74. Lest anyone think Nāgārjuna is somehow suggesting here that a ruler should not be inclined toward decisive action, nothing could be further from the truth. He is simply pointing out the necessity of deep reflection in formulating policy. Well implemented, this advice equips the ruler to respond not just rapidly, but also wisely.
75. This list is highly praised in other writings by Nāgārjuna where it is known as "the four bases of meritorious qualities" (四功德處). He discusses this list in his commentary on the ten bodhisattva grounds, in his commentary on the *Great Perfection of Wisdom Sutra*, and also in his *Bodhisaṃbhāra Śāstra*. Incidentally, these four factors are also described by the Buddha in the Āgamas (T01.0001.51a) and are also found in the *Vibhāṣa Śāstra* (T28.1547.419a), just two examples of non-Mahāyāna sources.
76. There are at least two noteworthy implications here: a) One shouldn't commit karmic errors simply for the sake of enjoying particular pleasures in this present life; and b) If one wants to have the happiness in the present which itself depends on the confidence that one will not have to suffer negative retributions in the future, one should therefore avoid committing karmic errors.
77. It is not the intention of this *śloka* to incite a state of constant fearfulness about the future. Rather it is to encourage constant vigilance regarding one's actions in the present, lest one create a fearsome karmic future through recklessly committing negative deeds bound to involve disastrous future retribution.
78. We do not know precisely which sort of "gaming" is really being referred to here, not least because this part of the chapter has no surviving Sanskrit versions. Paramārtha (or his editors) rendered it into Chinese as *weiqi* (圍棋), "encirclement chess," the ancient Chinese antecedent of what is now known in Japan and the West as the board game of "go." But Nāgārjuna's characterization makes it clear he is referring specifically to those types of competitive gaming or gambling objectionable because they encourage the growth of negative personal attributes. Hence I chose to render the English as "competitive gaming," which more readily calls to mind gambling games like poker. This seems to be more likely what Nāgārjuna intended than the polite intellectual parlor game we know as "chess" in the West. However, the articulated principle would seem to also rule out playing chess for money, a practice which is really not so common.
79. As this work is directly addressed to a male sovereign, the subject of these "impurity" contemplations is the nature of a woman's body when seen in the light of conventional truth. (At the level of ultimate truth, "pure" and "impure" are no longer valid categories.) In the case of the female Dharma student who is studying this work, it would be

most appropriate to direct such contemplations at the body of man, drawing similar conclusions with regard to it as Nāgārjuna is encouraging the King to draw regarding the body of a woman.

80. "Red and white effluents" are references to semen and menses.

81. "Inward" and "outward" are in essence Buddhist technical terms rooted in the Sanskrit which refer to "oneself" (in the case of the former) and to "others" (in the case of the latter). Because they may at times also refer to the standard literal connotations of these words in English, one can't so easily make the translated terms modularly default to the figurative sense usually intended by the Indian text.

82. This passage may seem obscure to those unaware of the multi-lifetime karmic effects of killing karma or the absence thereof. Such karma, even when merely residual, tends to make its perpetrator feared by others, this even on a subtle psychic level completely independent of the current presence or absence of an outwardly threatening appearance. An illustration of this is found in the story of the Buddha's shadow being able to quiet a terrified pigeon chased by a hawk whilst Śāriputra's shadow exerted no such calming effect. (See my anthology of tales told by Nāgārjuna, *Marvelous Stories from the Perfection of Wisdom* wherein the story from the *Mahāprajñāpāramitā Upadeśa* is translated [大智度論 / T25.1509.138c-d].)

83. This *śloka*, too, may seem obscure. The prayers of the farmers in the analogy are for the prospect that the dryness and insufferable heat will go away. This is simply an analogy for the wish that beings have that the person with hunting karma will just go away and relieve them of the oppressively menacing presence of his evil karmic energy.

84. The thirty-two major marks and eighty subsidiary characteristics of a buddha's body may seem to verge on mythic for those who have never encountered a buddha, this not least because of the highly metaphoric language of this class of early Buddhist scripture. It's perhaps most useful therefore for the Dharma student to focus primarily on incorporating the causal practices as recommended by Nāgārjuna, while letting the inevitably positive downstream karmic and corporal effects take care of themselves.

85. This is another instance of specific listing of the bodhisattva's four means of attraction (*catuḥ-saṃgraha vastu*). (These were explained more fully in the note to *śloka* number thirty-three of this chapter.)

86. Pāramartha (or his Chinese editor) attempts to force two of the major marks into the fourth foot of the *śloka*, creating at first glance a somewhat misleading sense in the Chinese that the rounding of the shoulders is being compared to a *gan-fu* (甘浮), which appears to be one of his space-saving, one-off transliterations, apparently for the central

trunk of the banyan tree, the standard analogy for the appearance of a buddha's body. He seems to be trying to use the *yuan* (圓) twice, once to describe a buddha's shoulders, and once to describe the similarity of a buddha's body to the *nyagrodha*.

87. Given the indecipherability of *ni-qu* (匿瞿), probably one of Pāramartha's one-off short-hand transliterations inserted to fit the dense five-characters per *śloka*-foot format, I was forced here simply to fill in the standard description regarding a buddha's major marks as manifest in the jaws.
88. "Gentleness" renders the Sanskrit antecedent for the Chinese *hua* (滑): *ślakṣṇa*.
89. "Bodhisattva" here is a proper noun and specific term of reference used exclusively for a buddha-to-be in that very life wherein he is destined to realize the utmost, right, and perfect enlightenment. Hence the most recent historical Buddha born in Lumbini is often referred to in the canonical literature as "the Bodhisattva."
90. I emend here the text with a graphically-similar variant found in four other editions, this to correct an obvious scribal error which recorded *she* (舍) for what should be *han* (含). Although many Western students of Buddhism tend to most readily associate the Sanskrit word *āgama* with the basic Southern Tradition scriptures promoting the individual-liberation goal of arhatship, the term *āgama* is actually a much more general reference to a collection of traditional doctrines, precepts, or sacred works, hence the validity of Nāgārjuna's reference here to "the *āgama* scriptures of the Great Vehicle."
91. "Those still in training and those beyond training" is an aggregating technical term collectively referring to all of the stages of progress toward arhatship within the individual-liberation vehicle.
92. Although, in this instance, no variant is recorded in *Taisho*, I'm making the same obviously appropriate emendation of the Sanskrit transliteration for *āgama* as was made in the first *śloka* of this chapter, this by substituting *han* (含) for *she* (舍).
93. The "and so forth" of "Space and so forth, including earth, water, and fire…" is almost certainly intended to refer to the remaining unmentioned component members of the six elements discussed earlier. Hence "consciousness" and "wind" are intended as well.
94. The "two types of attachment" are: 1) attachment to the existence of "persons" (which are in fact devoid of any inherently real existence); 2) attachment to the existence of "dharmas" (mental or physical phenomena constituting aspects of conventional existence).
95. A *saṅghārāma* is a monastic dwelling. Hence "*saṅghārāmas* along the roads" is a reference to facilities for monks and nuns to stay in while

traveling. Perhaps then Nāgārjuna was suggesting the establishment of a system of monastic hostels.

96. One might wonder why Nāgārjuna refers to making available "provisions for the needs of 'beings'" instead of simply referring to "the people." As will become clear later in the text, he is counseling the King to be concerned not only about the welfare of humans, but also of all animal life as well. This would of course include beasts of burden such as oxen, elephants, and others prone to suffer hunger and thirst on the roads as they travel in service of their owners' needs for transport and such.

97. "The Great Community" is term used to reference the entire congregation of a Buddhist community.

98. Emendation: Adopting the variant (of 遣 for 遺) found in four other editions.

99. The stipulation of "eight" is the Pāramārtha translation's adaptation to an established form of Sixth-century Chinese governance.

100. Lest it not be obvious, this śloka focuses specifically on the two fundamental issues involved in practice of the Bodhisattva Path, namely benefit of both self and others, guided by the aim of universal liberation from karma-bound suffering in cyclic existence. Nāgārjuna makes it clear that concern with the welfare of others is an urgent matter not to be deferred.

101. The reference here is to the seven steps taken by the Buddha immediately on being born. The historical buddhas are referred to as "the Bodhisattva" when discussing any point in their lives prior to realization of the utmost, right, and perfect enlightenment.

102. This is simply a reference to the practice of facilitating marriage between lay couples. Nāgārjuna describes this in less ambiguous detail in his *Bodhisaṃbhāra Śāstra* wherein it is quite clear that it is marriage ceremonies which are the subject of discussion. By facilitating people's being able to gain lifelong possession of that which they desire "to have and to hold," one plants causes for being able "to have and to hold" in each and every life meritorious qualities conducive to success on the path to buddhahood. This is the function of *dhāraṇīs*.

103. This śloka seems to be a continued articulation of the "facilitation of marriage" advice to the king wherein Nāgārjuna suggests he devote due attention to lowering the economic bar traditional culture so often place in the path of prospective matrimonial partners.

104. "Beyond this, one must not show them any further kindness" might at first sound unduly harsh. Not so. Nāgārjuna is simply protecting the King from being exploited by an endless stream of low-life manipulators and con men seeking royal support for their ostensible holiness.

A strict "critical necessities only" policy helps protect both the King and the treasury from charlatans.
105. This is a euphemistic reference to refusing to support those whose actions do not accord with Dharma so as to minimize the degree to which they may negatively influence others with their corrupt ways.
106. "Pressure to the point of vexation" refers here to less comfortable teaching techniques such as out-and-out scolding through which one directly confronts the stubborn with the need to set aside wrong or unwholesome actions and cultivate good. In practice, this type of technique would be adopted only by an acknowledged guru or other very senior monk in the instruction of egregiously-misbehaving monks. With the possible exception of special cases involving very committed personal disciples, this sort of instruction would almost never be considered appropriate for members of the laity.
107. This is a specific reference to the "three kinds of wisdom": learning-derived wisdom; contemplation-derived wisdom; and meditation-derived wisdom.
108. Emendation: Adopting the variant (of 天 for 大) occurring in four other editions.
109. In his "Letter from a Friend" (*Suhṛllekha*), Nāgārjuna mentions a number of the unfortunate circumstances encountered by hungry ghosts, including: non-fulfillment of any need or craving; constant hunger and thirst; extremes of cold and heat; weariness; privation; bellies huge as mountains with throats as narrow as a needle; extreme ugliness; mouths ablaze with fire attracting a diet of flying insects; craving to eat excrement an drink urine whilst even that is unobtainable; the moon, when sought for coolness, burns them; the sun when sought for warmth freezes them; fruits disappear whenever they enter an orchard; streams dry up whenever they approach; and they endure immensely long lifetimes marked by constant privation.

Nāgārjuna states that these sufferings of the hungry ghosts arise from the karma of miserly covetousness and jealousy. This listing is extracted from the *ślokas* of my Guṇavarman translation. (For variations on this and other topics as presented in one of Nāgārjuna's most important works, see my translations of all three Chinese editions of the *Suhṛllekha* as rendered from different Sanskrit manuscripts by Tripiṭaka Masters Guṇavarman, Saṅghavarman, and Yijing between 450 CE and 700 CE.)

110. One may notice I've rendered what appears to be "inwardly" (*nei* – 內) as "personally." The Sanskrit antecedent, however, is *adhyātma*, which does not refer solely to one's "inward" mental life as the English term might imply. Because it really just means "with regard to oneself" (as

opposed to "others"), its semantic range is much broader, including not just one's thoughts and emotions, but also one's words, actions, and even one's possessions when contrasted with those of others.
111. "And others" refers to the various classes of Dharma-protecting ghosts and spirits.
112. "Form realm" here is a reference corresponding to the higher levels of the heavens.
113. Lest it be unclear, as just listed, the ten qualities gained from kindness are: 1) One is well-liked by gods, humans, and other beings; 2) One experiences joy both day and night; 3) One experiences bliss both day and night; 4) One is protected by gods, humans, and other beings; 5) One remains free of adversaries (or at least is not bothered by them); 6) One is not harmed by fire; 7) One is not harmed by poison; 8) One is not harmed by being beaten; 9) One gains material wealth effortlessly; 10) One may be reborn in the form-realm heavens.
114. The "eight difficulties" are: 1-3) Rebirth in the hells, among the hungry ghosts, or among animals; 4) Rebirth on the continent of Uttarakuru (where blissful retribution is so great, no one is inclined to cultivate the Path); 5) Rebirth in the long-life heavens (where, again, there is not motivation to renounce cyclic existence in favor of the Path); 6) Being born deaf, blind, or mute; 7) Being endowed with sharp worldly intelligence and eloquence (of the sort disdainful of spiritual priorities); 8) Being born before or after the Dharma reign of a buddha.
115. "Dharma patience," more easily understood as "patience with respect to dharmas" is one of the two basic types of patience. ("Patience with respect to beings" is the other.) Basically, it is a reference to the cultivation of patience with respect to inward and outward aspects of existence such as heat, cold, hunger, thirst, desire, anger, delusion, praise, blame, pleasure, pain, success, failure, and so forth.

"Comprehensive retention" or "complete retention" is an approximate English translation of the Sanskrit *dhāraṇī*. *Dhāraṇīs* confer on the practitioner the ability to perfectly retain all Dharma learning and ability acquired in previous lives with the result that, in ensuing lives, no aspect of Path development is lost. This allows one to pick up more-or-less precisely where one left off in one's previous life cultivation of the Path. *Dhāraṇīs* are often identified with the cultivation of mantras. However, the power of *dhāraṇī* is not exclusively associated with mantras by any means. Nāgārjuna devotes a long discussion to this topic in his extensive commentary on the *Mahāprajñāpāramitā Sutra*. My translation of Nāgārjuna's *dhāraṇī* discussion should become available soon under separate cover.
116. This is most likely a reference to the five precepts and the five types

of fearlessness which they bestow on other beings. (Given the context, the list suggested in the Tibetan commentaries [sugar or molasses, ghee, honey, sesame oil, salt] seems somewhat improbable at least in terms of Paramārtha's use in the Chinese edition of the term: "five types of genuine giving." Note: There is no known extant Sanskrit for this śloka.)

A particularly relevant citation is found in the Āgamas (T02.125.648a) wherein observance of the five precepts is likened to "five types of great giving." These five are also given in the *Upāsaka Precepts Sutra* (優婆塞戒經 / T24.1488.1064a) where they are also expressly called "the five types of great giving," wherein they are equated with the giving of fearlessness directly alluded to by Nāgārjuna in this śloka, and wherein it is said that the most supreme form of giving is this giving of fearlessness as implicitly inherent in observance of the five precepts. The principle: When one takes on the five moral-virtue precepts, all beings one encounters are straightaway given the gift of not needing to fear that one will make them victims of one's killing, stealing, lying, sexual recklessness, or intoxicant-driven negative behaviors.

Nāgārjuna himself specifically equates precept observance with the giving of fearlessness in extensive discussions of the six perfections elsewhere in his corpus, most notably in the *Mahāprajñāpāramitā Upadeśa* where he notes how the perfection of moral virtue generates the perfection of giving (大智度論 / T25.1509.162b). (See my complete translation of that 14-chapter six perfections section under separate cover as "Nāgārjuna on the Six Perfections.")

For those wishing to incidentally contemplate another list of five types of genuine giving with a slightly different approach also employed by Nāgārjuna, there is the one attributed to the Buddha in the Āgamas which we find in the *Compendium of Essentials from the Scriptures* (諸經要集 / T54.2123.91c). There we have five types of superior giving classified according to the recipient (those coming from afar, those preparing to go a great distance, those who are sick, those who are hungry, and those who are knowledgeable about the Dharma).

117. Emendation: Adopting the variant (of 漏 for 流) occurring in four other editions.
118. Emendation: Adopting the variant (of 狹 for 陿) occurring in four other editions.
119. "Inspiring awe," more literally translated, would be rendered here as "hair-raising."
120. Because Paramārtha used multiple Chinese verse lines to render a few of the Sanskrit ślokas in this chapter, those extended-length śloka renderings are marked as 19a, 19b, etc. In some cases (as with 19b)

there is a degree of non-correspondence with the extant fragmentary Sanskrit or the Tibetan composite text. Existing data is insufficient to judge whether or not these cases involve commentarial interpolations in the Chinese or instead indicate material lost from a common ancestor text of the much later Sanskrit and Tibetan editions.

121. The intent of "purity from all four standpoints" is uncertain. It probably refers to the necessity of those in public service to ensure that everything they do is "pure" in four senses:

1) As regards the objective facts involved in the action;

2) As regards intent (i.e., not involving the exploitation of some "loophole");

3) As regards outward appearance (i.e. Don't adjust your hat in someone's apple orchard nor tie your shoes in someone's strawberry patch); and

4) As regards how someone with malicious intent might somehow be able to misconstrue to other rumor-mongers what actually occurred.

(These are just my "educated guesses" issuing from the ethical perspective of a monastic.)

122. The stipulation of "eight people" in "eight cabinet-level positions" may be an adaptation to Chinese governance customs. In any case, this is not found in either the Sanskrit or Tibetan texts.

123. "Twelve-part cycle" and "four skillful means" have no correlate in the Sanskrit or Tibetan. The former may be a reference to the twelve months of the year to which governments adjust in dealing with agriculture, monsoons, periodic flooding, disaster relief, and so forth. "Skillful means" in a Buddhist context usually refers to departures from the ideal adapted to the exigencies of circumstances, but still adhering to ethics and right principles.

124. Nāgārjuna's warning that evil will constantly flow forth from any circumstance wherein the ruler fails to ensure the rights of a prisoner likely refers to both the personal and societal effects which most likely will unfold from that single case. On the one hand, such reckless disregard of the principles of fairness and compassion is a harbinger of personal moral downfall. On the other, it is also this very sort of action which initiates intractable political opposition to the throne, this on the part of associates and sympathizers of those who have been egregiously wronged.

125. "Employing eyes investigating the purity of people's actions" is almost certainly a euphemism for use of intelligence agents vigilant about matters bearing on state security and the King's personal security. Presumably, they would be charged to report directly to the King, bypassing even his own regular personal security staff.

Translation Endnotes 217

Although one might wonder if Nāgārjuna isn't perhaps unnecessarily encouraging paranoia on the King's part, anyone who reads Indian political history will note the seemingly endless string of fratricides, patricides, regicides, and such which would make precautions of this sort very nearly essential. One will notice that Nāgārjuna at least counsels that such internal security operations be undertaken in accordance with the law.

126. Emendation: Adopting the Sanskrit-attested variant (of 魚 for 愚) found in four other editions.

Nāgārjuna is simply pointing out to the King in this passage that the classic monarchical brute force mode used by despots ("big fish eats little fish") is not inevitable, i.e. the King actually has the option of staying happily in power through enlightened policies and exemplary personal behaviors admired and supported by a moderately happy population.

127. Again, the implications here are two-fold: The King may beget his own karmic downfall by personally violating standards of personal behavior known to him through Dharma or, alternatively, he may fall through any outward actions he might take to interfere with the flourishing of right Dharma practice within his royal domain.

128. Emendation: Adopting the variant (of 苦 for 若) occurring in four other editions.

129. In spite of having mentioned in an earlier *śloka* that kingship is not something one can carry to a future life, Nāgārjuna is here instructing the King on how to do precisely that, this through the judicious implementation of enlightened personal behavior and royal policy.

130. The mind can *only* take as objective conditions already-past characteristics of sense objects. This perceptual phenomenon is not unlike the case of a high-flying rocket or jet plane the presence of which we may only be able to deduce by observing the contrail left in the wake of its passage. Nāgārjuna provides the fine and yet-more-vivid analogy of the image of the "wheel" one observes with the twirling of a firebrand in the dark which is, after all, not the firebrand itself, but rather only a visual image left in its wake distinguished by the mind with the perception: "circle of fire."

Regarding *śloka* 53c-d, having focused on the already-past characteristics of the given sense object, the mind may then make discriminations about the sense data, form some perception-based "opinion" about it such as "desirable," and then, in essence, "manufacture" (through false imputation) some experience of "bliss" which is actually more related to the false imputation itself than it is to the now already-past sense object.

The Chinese character I have translated as "lovely" here is *jing* (

淨) which is more usually translated as "pure." However, its use as a Chinese translation of the Sanskrit *śubha* ("splendid," "lovely," etc.) is well-known, especially as regards imputed qualities of the human body wherein it is the character most commonly used in translating the lust-defeating contemplation on the "loveliness" versus "unloveliness" (read "desirability" versus "undesirability") of the human body.

131. "The sense faculty's engagement with sense objects is the same" in the sense that this involves the same sort of erroneous perception as when the eye, through erroneous perception, sees a "circle" of fire associated with a twirling firebrand.

132. Emendation: Although no variants are listed in *Taisho*, there is an obvious scribal error here which involved the accidental substitution of 非 for the graphically similar 亦. Transcribing from a printing made from deteriorated woodblocks, this error could easily occur. This clause would make no sense in the absence of the correction.

133. Emendation: There was an obvious scribal error here involving the substitution of 離 for the graphically similar 雜. This is doubly obvious because the identical argument was made earlier in the refutation of the existence of the elements. As printed in *Taisho*, the statement would make no sense. Hence the correction.

134. The *śloka* makes two points which may not be entirely obvious if not explained more completely:

    1) If any ostensibly desirable object or circumstance is correctly perceived in terms of that "gate of liberation" known as "signlessness," it is straightaway realized to have no genuine inherent existence. This realization neutralizes any imputations through which that object or circumstance might be deemed "desirable." Consequently the mind ceases all attachment to that object and one becomes freed from that particular craving.

    2) Through contemplating the "non-arising" of suffering, one notices that "suffering" is in fact not a real dharma, is merely the product of self-generated imputations imposed on discrete and unconnected mind-moments, and has no genuine power by which it should be allowed to move one's thoughts either toward aversion or toward attraction. As a consequence, the desire to avoid circumstances involving suffering is caused to cease.

135. "Its dominance" is a reference to the dominant popularity of the Great Vehicle.

136. Emendation: Adopting the variant (of 昔 for 首) occurring in four other editions.

137. Emendation: Although no variants are listed in *Taisho*, there is an

obvious scribal error here which involved the accidental substitution of *le* (樂) for the graphically-similar *yao* (藥).

138. Here, as elsewhere in the text, it is not always certain whether Nāgārjuna's refutations are directed at classic wrong views in vogue at that time or whether they are directed at the King's own previously stated wrong views. In many places in the text, it is clear that Nāgārjuna is addressing the former, though one shouldn't rule out the possibility that both possibilities are true.

139. "Supreme Vehicle" is a reference to the Mahāyāna.

140. This may well be a reference to a story told by Nāgārjuna elsewhere of Śāriputra's amazement at the effect of the Buddha's countless lifetimes of moral virtue (大智度論 / T25.1509.138c-d). This effect became apparent one day when the Buddha, followed by Śāriputra, was walking along and encountered a squawking pigeon fleeing a hawk. When the Buddha's shadow fell upon the pigeon, it was immediately and entirely calmed. When the Buddha's shadow had passed, the pigeon commenced to squawk again in terror. When Śāriputra's shadow then fell upon the pigeon, no such calming effect occurred. Śāriputra then inquired about this, whereupon the Buddha explained a few things to Śāriputra, pointing out aspects of a buddha's knowledge well beyond the cognitive abilities of Śāriputra or any other arhat. (See my anthology of tales told by Nāgārjuna, *Marvelous Stories from the Perfection of Wisdom*, wherein I have translated this story from the *Mahāprajñāpāramitā Upadeśa*.)

141. Lest the meaning seem obscure, Nāgārjuna is pointing out to the King the extreme karmic consequences that would unfold to him were he to use the power of his throne to dictate proscription of anything in the Buddhist Canon.

142. The four reliances as listed by Nāgārjuna in the *Mahāprajñāpāramitā Upadeśa*: "As the Buddha told the Bhikshus when he was about to enter nirvāṇa, 'From this day on, you should rely upon the Dharma and not rely on any particular person. You should rely on the meaning and not rely on just the words. You should rely on wisdom and not rely merely on consciousness. You should rely on scriptures proclaiming the ultimate meaning and not rely on those which describe only provisional teachings.'" (大智度論 / T25.1509.125a-b).

143. "Truths" refers to the four truths. "Auxiliary Path factors" refers to the thirty-seven wings of enlightenment.

   Nāgārjuna is not claiming here that those teachings are in any way irrelevant for the bodhisattva. On the contrary, he insists in other works that such teachings are essential even for the bodhisattva, this because they are a means for staying aligned with the renunciant

Path even across the course of so many lifetimes devoted to universal-enlightenment priorities.

However, as cued in the second and third foot of this *śloka*, the way that the four truths and thirty-seven wings are cultivated in the context of the Bodhisattva Path is different from the way they are cultivated in the aspirational frame of the Small Vehicle's individual-liberation focus. In brief, the difference is in the wedding of these practices to the ever-renewed bodhisattva vow and perennial dedication to the bodhisattva's six perfections.

144. This is one of the major works on the Sanskrit language.
145. Emendation: Although no variants are listed in *Taisho*, there is an apparent scribal error here (as revealed by both the Sanskrit and the meaning of the *śloka*) which involved the accidental substitution of *shen* (深) for the graphically similar *kong* (空).
146. Giving, moral virtue, and patience are the first three of the six perfections. In the *Mahāprajñāpāramitā Upadeśa*, Nāgārjuna notes that these first three of the perfections figure most crucially in assembling the "bodhi provision" of merit, whereas the last three perfections (vigor, dhyāna meditation, and prajñā) figure most crucial in assembling the "bodhi provision" of wisdom. These are the two essential provisions essential for survival on and completion of the bodhisattva's path to buddhahood.

Nāgārjuna states elsewhere in that same text that the conditions of the householder's life are such that they are generally very conducive to production of merit, whereas those same conditions present a substantial challenge to rapid acquisition of highest wisdom, not least because deep dhyāna meditation is an essential prerequisite for developing genuine wisdom as opposed to the sort of facsimile wisdom which anyone can assemble through extensive reading of doctrine.
147. Beginning here, I include the numbering of *ślokas* in the Tibetan and Sanskrit after a backslash separating that number from the numbering of the verse-*śloka* units of the Chinese edition. There is some ambiguity in numbering later on in the chapter where, for most of the bodhisattva grounds, the assignment of attributes in the Chinese edition varies from that in the Tibetan edition and where the Chinese often contains attributes not present in the Tibetan edition. (Approximately 24 directly-related Sanskrit *ślokas* are no longer extant.) Any such *śloka*-numbering ambiguity will be signaled with the inclusion of an asterisk (*) in the suggested numbering schema, this where there is any significant variation in attributes or textual arrangement.
148. "Pratimokṣa" is a reference to the moral code for fully-ordained monastics. The meaning of the name itself (*prati*: "conducing toward."

mokṣa: "liberation.") is emblematic of the crucial role moral precepts play in gaining that liberation from karma-bound cyclic existence which is the goal of the Buddhist paths.

"Vinaya" is a general term for all traditional Buddhist moral codes and the secondary works explaining and discussing them. Vinaya is also inclusive of the moral precepts set down by the Buddha for the laity.

149. It is traditionally recommended that a newly-ordained monk or nun spend the first five years of his or her monastic career in fairly exclusive study of the moral codes and the works which discuss and explain them.

150. Lest one be confused by the fact that the text discusses fifty-nine mental factors when Nāgārjuna speaks of seven, it is only because the last seven components discussed collapse into a standard Buddhist list known as the "five hindrances." This is because two of the hindrances are "dual-component" hindrances long treated in Buddhist tradition as singular by both commentators and practitioners.

Specifically, I refer here to hindrances number three and number four, namely "lethargy-and-drowsiness" (*styāna-middha*) and "excitedness-and-regretfulness" (*auddhatya-kaukṛtya*). All standard traditional meditation manuals present these five hindrances as impediments to meditation which must be abandoned. In all cases, they are discussed in their "dual-component" form. Nāgārjuna does us the favor of briefly breaking these two apart into four, this for temporary didactic purposes, but still, he intends that we treat them in the standard way, as two dual-component hindrances, not as four. Hence the "fifty-nine" topics of discussion collapse into the "fifty-seven" to which he specifically refers in this *śloka*.

151. I'm including the Sanskrit equivalencies from the extant materials where I'm fairly certain about the correlation with these fifty-seven "delusions" as they are reflected in Paramārtha's Chinese. Where I fail to provide equivalencies, it is due to some tentativeness on my part as to whether the extant Sanskrit closely reflects the Sanskrit terms actually translated by Paramārtha.

152. Emendation: Although no variants are listed in *Taisho*, there is an obvious scribal error here wherein *guai* (怪) had been substituted at some point for *zeng* (憎), probably in recopying a deteriorated manuscript or recarving a chipped woodblock plate. The copyist probably read the text's "definition," interpreted it as meaning the graphically-similar *guai* (怪), and then made the substitution based on that. In any case, the emendation is supported by both Sanskrit and Tibetan editions. Additionally, Paramārtha uses *zeng* (憎) throughout the manuscript for most cases wherein "anger" or "hatred" are the intended

meaning.
153. The Chinese reads literally: "[Self]-intoxication."
154. One may care to note here that "arrogance" is, in most Buddhist dharmic taxonomies, one of the "root" afflictions, a standard listing of which consists of: covetousness, hatred, stupidity, arrogance, afflicted doubtfulness, and wrong views.

Also, the types of arrogance vary in their number and their analyses. The most common schemas list a numeric range between seven and ten. One will note that the text here seems to treat one major type and six subtypes as indicating a total of seven. Looking at the Sanskrit and Tibetan texts, one may be inclined to suspect that there has been an "extra" commentarial-interpolation śloka inserted into the Chinese text (between śloka 7 and śloka 8) which "adds in" a seventh subtype in the form of a second sort of "arrogance in inferiority" (*adhamo-māna*). That this additional subtype is mentioned here is owing to the fact that "arrogance in inferiority" comes in two versions: "outwardly directed" and "inwardly directed." The Sanskrit and Tibetan versions of the text only mention the "inwardly-directed" version (in śloka 12).

155. This is a śloka which could be thought of as representing an interpolated commentarial verse more-or-less "stepping in" to note the existence of this "outwardly-directed" subtype of the two types of "arrogance in inferiority." The other subtype of "arrogance in inferiority," the type which is exclusively "inwardly-directed," is treated in śloka 12, the sole location in which this one type among the seven types of arrogance is discussed in all language editions of the text (i.e. in the Sanskrit and Tibetan editions as well).

The rationale for inserting an interpolated śloka here may be that its putative author didn't think it was really proper to speak of one general type and six subtypes of arrogance as really constituting the "seven types" introduced as a topic at the end of śloka 6. Thus the insertion of the other type of "arrogance in inferiority" would legitimately produce a total of seven subtypes of arrogance, thus "restoring" completeness to the text which may never have included both subtypes of "arrogance in inferiority" in the first place.

It could also be that at some point along the line this "extra" śloka was carefully written alongside the regular text by some esteemed master of the Dharma, with the result that it was pulled directly into the text when it came time for recopying.

In any case, I am counting "arrogance in inferiority" only once for the purposes of according with Nāgārjuna's listing of 57 faults, doing so in the one place where it is certainly part of the text common to all three major traditions, namely in śloka 12.

156. The term *"upādāna-skandha"* is a reference to an association between

"grasping" or "appropriation" and the five aggregates (*skandhas* = form, feeling, perception, karmic formative factors, consciousness). This grasping is actually bivalent in the sense that the *skandhas* / aggregates are at the same time "appropriated" and also "appropriating."

I prefer to translate "appropriated" to reflect the metaphysical / ontological error closest to the root in generating the unnecessary suffering involved in human existence This problem of course is the universal tendency to seize upon the five aggregates as constituting a "person." In this sense they are "appropriated," this due to erroneously imputing person-hood on an artificial aggregation of disparate factors. Once "appropriated," then, of course, all manner of secondary "appropriating" unfolds from there, unleashing an endless cascade of karmic errors producing the karma-bound suffering we refer to as "cyclic existence."

157. One should note that two types of "arrogance in inferiority" are described. The first type (see eighth *śloka*) is "other-directed," whereas this second type is "self-directed."
158. "Extortion" or "intimidation" or "coercion" are all perhaps a bit too strong as translations for what may involve much subtler tactics than anything involving bald threats. In this instance, the victim is more likely to be manipulated into compliance and generosity through shaming him or otherwise making him feel bad about himself.
159. Although the meaning of the *doṣa* is clear enough in Chinese, its Sanskrit is not so easily extracted from the surviving Sanskrit fragments. Hence I have simply substituted the Sanskrit with an asterisk after the *doṣa* number (*) to signal the nature of the difficulty.
160. Emendation: Substituting *xiang* (想) for *xiang* (相) to correct an obvious scribal error. The emendation is corroborated by the extant Sanskrit. Additionally, this is a standard abhidharmic category not exclusive to this text.
161. For the two *doṣas* contained in this *śloka*, although the meanings of the *doṣas* are clear enough in the Chinese, their Sanskrit antecedents are not so easily extracted from the surviving Sanskrit fragments. Hence I have simply substituted the Sanskrit with an asterisk after the *doṣa* number (*) to signal the nature of the difficulty.
162. This "desire" is the first of the five hindrances which are specifically held to constitute obstacles to the development of meditative discipline (*dhyāna*).
163. "Nine causes and conditions" refers to three matters of concern which may have occurred in the past, may be occurring in the present, or perhaps may occur in the future. The three matters of concern are that some adversary might: 1) wreak harm on oneself; 2) wreak

harm on one's close relations; or 3) Be enjoying some benefit which one resents.

164. This "ill-will" is the second of the five hindrances.

165. This and the next together constitute the third of the five hindrances, "lethargy-and-drowsiness" (*styāna-middha*).

On the question of why "lethargy-and-drowsiness" is a dual-component hindrance, Vasubandhu indicates (in Chapter Five of his *Treatise on the Treasury of Analytic Knowledge*) that it is because both "lethargy" and "drowsiness" are nourished by the same five factors and are productive of the same result of mental languor. Pruden, *Abhidharma-kośa-bhāṣyam* (851-2).

166. This and the next together constitute the fourth of the five hindrances, "excitedness-and-regretfulness" (*auddhatya-kaukṛtya*).

On the question of why "excitedness-and-regretfulness" is a dual-component hindrance, Vasubandhu indicates (in Chapter Five of his *Treatise on the Treasury of Analytic Knowledge*) that it is because both "excitedness" and "regretfulness" are nourished by the same four factors, are starved by the same single factor (calmness), and are productive of the same result of mental agitation. Pruden, *Abhidharma-kośa-bhāṣyam* (852).

167. This "doubtfulness" is the fifth of the five hindrances.

168. Emendation: Adopting the variant (of 弈 for 今) occurring in four other editions.

169. The Sanskrit name for the first bodhisattva ground: *pramudita*.

170. Beginning here and extending on through the entire section devoted to describing the ten bodhisattva grounds, we have significant textual differences manifesting between the Chinese text and the two other editions, the Sanskrit and the Tibetan. (The Sanskrit is not extant for the last few grounds.) The Chinese adds more descriptive material when compared with the Sanskrit and Tibetan and differs as regards some of the attributes assigned to the grounds. Inconsistencies of this sort are signaled by my inclusion of an asterisk (*) in my *śloka* numbering schema.

171. The Sanskrit name for the second bodhisattva ground: *vimala*.

172. The ten different types of pure karma are just the path of the ten types of good karmic deeds. Specifically, these involve restraint from killing, stealing, sexual misconduct, lying, harsh speech, divisive speech, frivolous / lewd speech, covetousness, hatefulness, and wrong views, the first three being concerned with the body, the next four being concerned with mouth karma, and the last three being concerned with the quality of one's mental life.

173. The Sanskrit name for the third bodhisattva ground: *prabhākara*.

174. The Sanskrit name for the fourth bodhisattva ground: *arciṣmati*.
175. "Components of the Path," in addition to being a general reference to all of the practice techniques of the Mahāyāna, is also a specific reference to the thirty-seven wings of enlightenment.
176. The Sanskrit name for the fifth bodhisattva ground: *sudurjaya*.
177. The Sanskrit name for the sixth bodhisattva ground: *abhimukha*.
178. The Sanskrit name for the seventh bodhisattva ground: *dūraṃgama*.
179. "Virgin youth" (*kumāra*) and "Immovability" (*acala*) are two standard names for the eighth bodhisattva ground.
180. The "two types of benefit" are the bodhisattva's benefit of self and benefit of others.
181. The Sanskrit name for the ninth bodhisattva ground: *sādhumati*.
182. The four types of eloquence are: unobstructed eloquence through unlimited skill in expressing meanings; unobstructed eloquence through unlimited skill in drawing forth the various teaching dharmas; unobstructed eloquence through unlimited skill in artful phrasing; unobstructed eloquence consisting of unlimited delight in discoursing on the Dharma.
183. The four types of response: the direct response; the analytic response; the rhetorical-question response (often then followed with a contrary answer to the position seized on in replying to the rhetorical-question response); the response consisting in setting aside the question through silence (often used where the question is based on entirely false premises).
184. The Sanskrit of the tenth bodhisattva ground: *dharmamegha*.
185. The twenty ślokas appear as twenty-one "verses" in the Chinese, this because Paramārtha found it necessary to translate Sanskrit śloka number eighty-four with two Chinese verses.
186. Unless one is already a highly-realized bodhisattva or a buddha who is manifesting in a woman's body as a skillful means through which one works toward the liberation of other beings, it is held to be much more challenging when manifesting in a woman's body to achieve rapid acquisition of the higher reaches of the Path. Hence the wish that all who aspire to rapid path-progress will have the opportunity to avail themselves of the most efficient means for accomplishing the task.
187. Regarding the "clarities," the three clarities are: clarity with respect to past lives; clarity with respect to others' thoughts; clarity with respect to the ending of outflow defilements. As for "bases," this refers to completeness in merit and wisdom, the two provisions essential for the realization of buddhahood.

188. "At all points along the way" means "in each and every life." This is set up by making vows to that effect in this very life which one then renews regularly, preferably daily. This establishes extremely strong present life causes bound to produce the desired effect in future lives, given of course that the quality of one's karmic actions is adequately refined to support such auspicious rebirths.

189. Regarding: "May they thus be bound for certain success [on the path to] bodhi," "certain success" is an explicit reference to the "stage of certain success" (*samyaktva-niyāma*), a point of irreversibility on the Buddhist practitioner's chosen path of liberation. For those on the individual-liberation path wherein they aspire to arhatship, this is most directly associated with the path of seeing gained by the stream-winner.

    For those on the universal liberation path of the bodhisattva, the precise stage involved depends somewhat on the ultimacy of the grounds-schema referenced. (Provisional teachings and ultimate teachings may vary on this.) It is most typical I believe to find it associated with the eighth ground wherein one finally becomes so irreversibly bound toward buddhahood that not even the most eloquent non-Buddhist or arhat can turn one away to a lesser spiritual goal. Accordingly, we find Nāgārjuna himself stating in his *Ten Grounds Vibhāṣā*: "On the eighth ground, one's vows cannot be moved even by the heavenly demons, by Brahmā, by any śramaṇa, or by any brahman. It is on account of this that it is referred to as 'the ground of immovability' (*acala-bhūmi*)." (十住毘婆沙論 / T26.1521.23a)

190. The five superknowledges (*pañca-abhijñā*) are the heavenly eye, heavenly ear, knowledge of others' thoughts, knowledge of past lives, and psychic power.

191. Emendation: Substituting *zeng* 增 for *zeng* 憎. Although the two characters were often interchangeable in ancient times (as evidenced in the *Mozi* and the *Lunheng*), failure to use the obviously correct glyph in this context produces certain confusion due to the contradictory meanings in Buddhist literature of the two glyphs' more standard definitions.

192. "The most supreme station" is a reference to the most supreme level of spiritual development on any of the Buddhist paths. Hence this is a reference to complete realization of buddhahood.

193. Emending the text by substituting *guo* (過) for *guo* (果) to correct a scribal error probably originating in homophony. (This occurs when the woodblock carver or copyist holds the sound of an erroneous homophonous character in mind in an attempt to remember it whilst carving or writing a new character or sentence as he works on a new copy.)

The decision to emend is based on comparison with both the Sanskrit and Tibetan after noticing the incongruousness of the idea implicit in the Chinese as it stands. The Sanskrit is *doṣa* for which the Taisho text has *guo* (果) when it should have either *guo* (過) or *huo* (惑), both of which are standard translations for *doṣa* and both of which are partial homonyms of the erroneously-transmitted character, the former in initial, medial, and final (but not tone), the latter of which is homophonous in medial, final, and tone (but not initial). (I don't really think there's much point in giving any particular weight to "tone" inconsistencies in this sort of context, given the vintage of the text.)

In any case, it's also clear this change is warranted from the standpoint of mirrored parallelism as well. ("All faults" dispensed with in the first *śloka* foot is mirrored by "manifold qualities" taken on in the second *śloka* foot.)

194. Where a *doṣa's* meaning is clear enough in the Chinese, but the Sanskrit antecedent is not so easily extracted from the surviving Sanskrit fragment, I have simply substituted the Sanskrit with an asterisk (*) to signal the nature of the difficulty.

SOURCE TEXT VARIANT READINGS

[0493005] 〔一卷〕－【宋】【元】【明】【宮】 [0493006] 三藏＋（法師）【宋】【元】【明】【宮】 [0493007] 後＝復【宋】【元】【明】【宮】 [0493008] 或＝惑【宋】【元】【明】【宮】 [0493009] 遭＝連【宋】【元】【明】【宮】 [0493010] 恒＝怪【宋】【元】【明】【宮】 [0493011] 聰＝聽【元】【明】【宮】 [0494001] 實＝寶【明】 [0494002] 芽＝牙【宋】【元】【宮】 [0494003] 旋＝捉【宮】 [0494004] 起＝死【明】 [0494005] 受＝愛【宋】【元】【明】【宮】下同	正體字
[0493005] 〔一卷〕－【宋】【元】【明】【宮】 [0493006] 三藏＋（法师）【宋】【元】【明】【宮】 [0493007] 后＝复【宋】【元】【明】【宮】 [0493008] 或＝惑【宋】【元】【明】【宮】 [0493009] 遭＝连【宋】【元】【明】【宮】 [0493010] 恒＝怪【宋】【元】【明】【宮】 [0493011] 聪＝听【元】【明】【宮】 [0494001] 实＝宝【明】 [0494002] 芽＝牙【宋】【元】【宮】 [0494003] 旋＝捉【宮】 [0494004] 起＝死【明】 [0494005] 受＝爱【宋】【元】【明】【宮】下同	简体字

正體字	[0494006] 今＝令【元】【明】【宮】 [0494007] 信＝何【元】 [0494008] 已＝色【宋】【元】【明】【宮】 [0494009] 念＝多【宋】【元】【明】【宮】 [0495001] 智＝聖【明】 [0495002] 不自＝自不【明】 [0495003] 雜＝離【宋】＊【元】＊【明】＊［＊1］ [0495004] 業＝等【宋】【元】【明】【宮】 [0495005] 及諸＝諸及【宋】【元】【明】【宮】 [0495006] 〔寶行王正論〕－【明】＊［＊1 2］ [0495007] 拆蕉＝析樵【宋】【元】【明】【宮】 [0495008] 拆＝析【宋】【元】【明】【宮】 [0495009] 像＝象【宋】【元】【宮】 [0495010] 約＝幻【宋】【元】【明】【宮】 [0495011] 誰＝離【宋】【元】【明】
简体字	[0494006] 今＝令【元】【明】【宫】 [0494007] 信＝何【元】 [0494008] 已＝色【宋】【元】【明】【宫】 [0494009] 念＝多【宋】【元】【明】【宫】 [0495001] 智＝圣【明】 [0495002] 不自＝自不【明】 [0495003] 杂＝离【宋】＊【元】＊【明】＊［＊1］ [0495004] 业＝等【宋】【元】【明】【宫】 [0495005] 及诸＝诸及【宋】【元】【明】【宫】 [0495006] 〔宝行王正论〕－【明】＊［＊1 2］ [0495007] 拆蕉＝析樵【宋】【元】【明】【宫】 [0495008] 拆＝析【宋】【元】【明】【宫】 [0495009] 像＝象【宋】【元】【宫】 [0495010] 约＝幻【宋】【元】【明】【宫】 [0495011] 谁＝离【宋】【元】【明】

[0496001]	住＝信【明】下同	
[0496002]	說＝欲【明】	
[0496003]	執＝說【宮】	
[0496004]	汝＝如【明】	
[0496005]	主＝生【宮】	
[0496006]	憎＝增【宋】【元】【明】【宮】＊	
[0496007]	命＝朋【宋】【元】【明】【宮】	
[0496008]	德＝得【宋】【元】【明】【宮】	正體字
[0496009]	信＝住【明】	
[0496010]	靜＝靖【宮】	
[0496011]	臭＝嗅【宋】【元】【明】	
[0496012]	身＝事【明】	
[0496013]	泼＝沃【宋】【元】【明】【宮】	
[0497001]	權＝摧【宮】	
[0497002]	汰＝伏【宋】【元】【明】	
[0496001]	住＝信【明】下同	
[0496002]	说＝欲【明】	
[0496003]	执＝说【宮】	
[0496004]	汝＝如【明】	
[0496005]	主＝生【宮】	
[0496006]	憎＝增【宋】【元】【明】【宮】＊	
[0496007]	命＝朋【宋】【元】【明】【宮】	
[0496008]	德＝得【宋】【元】【明】【宮】	简体字
[0496009]	信＝住【明】	
[0496010]	静＝靖【宮】	
[0496011]	臭＝嗅【宋】【元】【明】	
[0496012]	身＝事【明】	
[0496013]	泼＝沃【宋】【元】【明】【宮】	
[0497001]	权＝摧【宮】	
[0497002]	汰＝伏【宋】【元】【明】	

正體字	[0497003] 膊＝腨【宋】【元】【明】【宮】 [0497004] 養＝食【元】【明】 [0497005] 竪＝堅【明】 [0497006] 逎＝道【宋】【元】【明】【宮】 [0497007] 阿舍＝阿含【宋】【元】【明】【宮】＊ [0498001] 善＝苦【宋】【元】【明】【宮】 [0498002] 寶＝實【明】 [0498003] 畫＝盡【明】 [0498004] 色＝急【宋】【元】【明】【宮】 [0498005] 綖＝線【宋】【元】【明】【宮】 [0498006] 莖＝筳【宋】【元】【明】【宮】 [0498007] 酥＝蘇【宋】【元】【明】【宮】 [0498008] 盤＝槃【宋】【元】【明】【宮】 [0499001] 債＝匱【宋】【元】【明】【宮】 [0499002] 遺＝遣【宋】【元】【明】【宮】	
简体字	[0497003] 膊＝腨【宋】【元】【明】【宮】 [0497004] 养＝食【元】【明】 [0497005] 竪＝坚【明】 [0497006] 逎＝道【宋】【元】【明】【宮】 [0497007] 阿舍＝阿含【宋】【元】【明】【宮】＊ [0498001] 善＝苦【宋】【元】【明】【宮】 [0498002] 宝＝实【明】 [0498003] 画＝尽【明】 [0498004] 色＝急【宋】【元】【明】【宮】 [0498005] 綖＝线【宋】【元】【明】【宮】 [0498006] 莖＝筳【宋】【元】【明】【宮】 [0498007] 酥＝苏【宋】【元】【明】【宮】 [0498008] 盘＝盘【宋】【元】【明】【宮】 [0499001] 债＝匮【宋】【元】【明】【宮】 [0499002] 遗＝遣【宋】【元】【明】【宮】	

Source Text Variant Readings

[0499003] 捨＝修【明】	
[0499004] 於＝施【明】【宮】＊［＊ 1］	
[0499005] 大＝天【宋】【元】【明】【宮】	
[0499006] 奉＝敬【宋】【元】【明】【宮】	
[0499007] 杖＝仗【宋】【元】【明】【宮】	
[0500001] 蟲＝螺【宋】【元】【明】【宮】	
[0500002] 流＝漏【宋】【元】【明】【宮】	正體字
[0500003] 供＝借【宋】【元】【明】【宮】	
[0500004] 陜＝狹【宋】【元】【明】【宮】	
[0500005] 王＝心【元】【明】【宮】	
[0500006] 后＝舌【宮】	
[0500007] 在＝存【宮】	
[0500008] 隻＝侯【宋】【元】【明】	
[0500009] 常＝當【元】【明】	
[0500010] 月月＝日日【宋】【元】【明】【宮】	
[0499003] 舍＝修【明】	
[0499004] 于＝施【明】【宮】＊［＊ 1］	
[0499005] 大＝天【宋】【元】【明】【宮】	
[0499006] 奉＝敬【宋】【元】【明】【宮】	
[0499007] 杖＝仗【宋】【元】【明】【宮】	
[0500001] 蠱＝螺【宋】【元】【明】【宮】	
[0500002] 流＝漏【宋】【元】【明】【宮】	简体字
[0500003] 供＝借【宋】【元】【明】【宮】	
[0500004] 陕＝狹【宋】【元】【明】【宮】	
[0500005] 王＝心【元】【明】【宮】	
[0500006] 后＝舌【宮】	
[0500007] 在＝存【宮】	
[0500008] 只＝侯【宋】【元】【明】	
[0500009] 常＝当【元】【明】	
[0500010] 月月＝日日【宋】【元】【明】【宮】	

正體字	[0501001] 於＝立【明】 [0501002] 悲＝非【宋】【元】【明】【宮】 [0501003] 莊＝粧【明】 [0501004] 思＝恩【宋】【元】【明】【宮】 [0501005] 王＝玉【明】 [0501006] 刺＝辣【宋】【元】【明】【宮】 [0501007] 愚＝魚【宋】【元】【明】【宮】 [0501008] 若＝苦【宋】【元】【明】【宮】 [0501009] 到＝倒【宋】【元】【明】【宮】 [0501010] 根＝緣【明】 [0501011] 離＝維【明】 [0501012] 體＝離【明】 [0501013] 一＝二【明】 [0501014] 乘＝乖【宋】【元】【明】【宮】 [0501015] 幻＝約【明】
简体字	[0501001] 于＝立【明】 [0501002] 悲＝非【宋】【元】【明】【宮】 [0501003] 庄＝粧【明】 [0501004] 思＝恩【宋】【元】【明】【宮】 [0501005] 王＝玉【明】 [0501006] 刺＝辣【宋】【元】【明】【宮】 [0501007] 愚＝鱼【宋】【元】【明】【宮】 [0501008] 若＝苦【宋】【元】【明】【宮】 [0501009] 到＝倒【宋】【元】【明】【宮】 [0501010] 根＝缘【明】 [0501011] 离＝维【明】 [0501012] 体＝离【明】 [0501013] 一＝二【明】 [0501014] 乘＝乖【宋】【元】【明】【宮】 [0501015] 幻＝约【明】

[0501016]	觀＝信【明】	
[0502001]	來＝能【明】	
[0502002]	首＝昔【宋】【元】【明】【宮】	
[0502003]	小乘＝乘小【宮】	
[0502004]	性＝往【元】	
[0502005]	惑＝或【宋】下同【元】下同【明】下同	
[0502006]	不＝下【宋】【元】【明】【宮】	正
[0503001]	今＝令【宋】【元】【明】【宮】	體
[0503002]	辱＝度【宋】【元】【明】【宮】	字
[0503003]	作＝修【宋】【元】【明】【宮】	
[0504001]	真＝奠【明】	
[0504002]	間＝聞【明】	
[0504003]	王＝主【宋】【元】【明】【宮】	
[0504004]	作＝行【宮】	
[0504005]	辦＝辨【宋】【元】，＝辯【明】【宮】	
[0501016]	观＝信【明】	
[0502001]	来＝能【明】	
[0502002]	首＝昔【宋】【元】【明】【宮】	
[0502003]	小乘＝乘小【宮】	
[0502004]	性＝往【元】	
[0502005]	惑＝或【宋】下同【元】下同【明】下同	
[0502006]	不＝下【宋】【元】【明】【宮】	简
[0503001]	今＝令【宋】【元】【明】【宮】	体
[0503002]	辱＝度【宋】【元】【明】【宮】	字
[0503003]	作＝修【宋】【元】【明】【宮】	
[0504001]	真＝奠【明】	
[0504002]	间＝闻【明】	
[0504003]	王＝主【宋】【元】【明】【宮】	
[0504004]	作＝行【宮】	
[0504005]	办＝辨【宋】【元】，＝辩【明】【宮】	

正體字

[0504006] 莊＝壯【明】
[0504007] 所＝作【明】
[0504008] 萬＝方【元】【明】
[0504009] 量＝盡【宋】【元】【明】【宮】
[0505001] 〔一卷〕－【宋】【元】【明】

简体字

[0504006] 庄＝壯【明】
[0504007] 所＝作【明】
[0504008] 万＝方【元】【明】
[0504009] 量＝尽【宋】【元】【明】【宮】
[0505001] 〔一卷〕－【宋】【元】【明】

About the Translator

Bhikshu Dharmamitra (ordination name "Heng Shou"— 釋恆授) is a Chinese-tradition translator-monk and one of the early American disciples (since 1968) of the late Weiyang Ch'an patriarch, Dharma teacher, and exegete, the Venerable Master Hsuan Hua (宣化上人). He has a total of 23 years in robes during two periods as a monastic (1969–1975; 1991 to present).

Dharmamitra's principal educational foundations as a translator lie in four years of intensive monastic training and Chinese-language study of classic Mahāyāna texts in a small-group setting under Master Hua from 1968–1972, undergraduate Chinese language study at Portland State University, a year of intensive one-on-one Classical Chinese study at the Fu Jen University Language Center near Taipei, and two years of study at the University of Washington's School of Asian Languages and Literature (1988–90).

Since taking robes again under Master Hua in 1991, Dharmamitra has devoted his energies primarily to study and translation of classic Mahāyāna texts with a special interest in works by Ārya Nāgārjuna and related authors. To date, he has translated a dozen important texts, most of which are slated for publication by Kalavinka Press.

Kalavinka Buddhist Classics Title List

Meditation Instruction Texts

The Essentials of Buddhist Meditation
A marvelously complete classic *śamathā-vipaśyanā* (calming-and-insight) meditation manual. By Tiantai Śramaṇa Zhiyi (538–597 CE).

Six Gates to the Sublime
The earliest Indian Buddhist meditation method explaining the essentials of breath and calming-and-insight meditation. By Śramaṇa Zhiyi.

Bodhisattva Path Texts

Nāgārjuna on the Six Perfections
Chapters 17–30 of Ārya Nāgārjuna's *Mahāprājñāpāramitā Upadeśa*.

Marvelous Stories from the Perfection of Wisdom
130 stories from Ārya Nāgārjuna's *Mahāprājñāpāramitā Upadeśa*.

A Strand of Dharma Jewels (Ārya Nāgārjuna's *Ratnāvalī*)
The earliest extant edition, translated by Paramārtha: *ca* 550 CE

Nāgārjuna's Guide to the Bodhisattva Path
The *Bodhisaṃbhāra Treatise* with abridged Vaśitva commentary.

The Bodhisaṃbhāra Treatise Commentary
The complete exegesis by the Indian Bhikshu Vaśitva (*ca* 300–500 CE).

Letter from a Friend - The Three Earliest Editions
The earliest extant editions of Ārya Nāgārjuna's *Suhṛlekkha*:
Translated by Tripiṭaka Master Guṇavarman   (*ca* 425 CE)
Translated by Tripiṭaka Master Saṅghavarman   (*ca* 450 CE)
Translated by Tripiṭaka Master Yijing   (*ca* 675 CE)

Resolve-for-Enlightenment Texts

On Generating the Resolve to Become a Buddha
On the Resolve to Become a Buddha by Ārya Nāgārjuna
Exhortation to Resolve on Buddhahood by Patriarch Sheng'an Shixian
Exhortation to Resolve on Buddhahood by the Tang Literatus, Peixiu

Vasubandhu's Treatise on the Bodhisattva Vow
By Vasubandhu Bodhisattva (*ca* 300 CE)

*All Kalavinka Press translations include facing-page source text.

www.ingramcontent.com/pod-product-compliance
Lightning Source LLC
LaVergne TN
LVHW040736250326
834688LV00031B/321